UNTOLD
PARIS

*For Marie-Dominique, Louise
and my French family.*

JOHN BAXTER

UNTOLD
PARIS

The Secret History of
the City of Light

F FRANCES
LINCOLN

CONTENTS

IN THE SHADOWS

WAYS OF LIFE

"PARIS WAS AROUND US AND HOW COULD IT BE ALIEN IN OUR MINDS AND HEARTS EVEN IF NO FRENCHMAN EVER SPOKE TO US? WHAT IT OFFERED TO US WAS WHAT IT HAD OFFERED TO MEN FROM OTHER COUNTRIES FOR HUNDREDS OF YEARS; IT WAS A LIGHTED PLACE WHERE THE IMAGINATION WAS FREE."

MORLEY CALLAGHAN, *THAT SUMMER IN PARIS*, 1963

INTRODUCTION

I came to Paris more than thirty years ago with only one aim – to marry the woman I loved. Having achieved this, I looked for other ways of keeping busy. There was my writing – but writing, contrary to the popular imagination, doesn't take up a lot of time. *Thinking* of what to write: that can devour decades – look at Marcel Proust. But while one is thinking, it helps to be doing something else.

The French have a phrase to cover 'something else'. They call it *un violon d'Ingres* (Ingres' violin). The painter Jean-Auguste-Dominique Ingres was also a pianist and amateur composer. His friends humoured him and attended his musical evenings – Franz Liszt grudgingly called his playing 'charming' – but his true talents lay elsewhere. Out of this emerged the term *violon d'Ingres* for any activity carried on by someone more accomplished in another field.

I needed to find such an activity. But then it found me.

A friend asked for my help running an annual writers' seminar. People came from all over the world to attend its intensive tutorials. As relief, we offered some diversions, including walks around sites of literary significance, for which we hired local academics. They did a good job. Mostly.

'He looked ideal,' my colleague said of the man we'd hired that year. She read me what some clients had written about his first walk: 'frankly boring' … 'not what we expected' … 'we didn't finish'.

'Well,' I said, 'we're stuck with him, it seems.'

'Not any more,' she said. 'I let him go.'

'Who's going to do the walks now?'

She looked at me pointedly.

'*Me?* I'm no guide. I wouldn't know where to start.'

'You've been on enough of these things. Just tell them some stories.'

'Well … let me think about it.'

'Think quickly,' she said. 'Your first walk's tomorrow at three.'

The following afternoon, I watched my group assemble. A bearded Scot, two Californian girls, forever whispering to each other, and three middle-aged women from the American Midwest with the indefinable mien that signalled 'school-teacher' – or maybe 'librarian'. Six, out of a possible fifty. Word had obviously got around.

'Perhaps we'd better start.' Then, almost shouting over the traffic noise, 'We're standing on rue de Vaugirard …'

Busy street corners, however, are no place to explain things. Words barely leave your lips before fading into the city din. I led them around the corner to a quieter side street, and encountered an additional problem. Looking around, I couldn't for the moment spot a single point of literary interest.

At this point, providence intervened. We'd stopped outside an antique shop. And in its window, prominently displayed, was a slim metal opium pipe.

Every pleasure creates a gadgetry as satisfying as the thing itself. Like golfers with their matched Bobby Jones woods or chefs with their Sabatier knives, serious *opiomanes* (opium addicts) competed to own the most richly decorated pipe, the correct lamp to heat the pellet of opium, the appropriate needle to hold it in the flame.

My fascination with the pipe must have been obvious, because the others joined me at the window.

'I don't understand how you smoke it,' said the Scot, peering at the pipe. 'I mean, it has no bowl.'

'... and were there really ...' asked one of the teachers, her voice hushed with a kind of wistfulness. '... opium *dens*?'

I looked around at attentive faces. Even the Valley girls had stopped gossiping.

'Dens?' I said. 'Yes, there were lots of them. Only they were called *fumeries*. There was a practical reason for them. And the pipe ... well, you take a little of the opium gum ...'

There, on that sunny afternoon, as shoppers and schoolkids and the odd tourist strolled by, we lifted a corner of the curtain that hid an addiction which enmeshed Jean Cocteau and Pablo Picasso and Charles Baudelaire. I tried to explain how the English love the sun while the French seek the shade. How opium offers no thrill, no high. Rather it's the key to a space *between* sensations, a weaving together of music, colour, light, and form ...

I barely murmured but they heard every word. What passed between us could not really be said. But it transformed us. No longer guide and party, we were conspirators.

A week later, as I crossed rue de Seine in front of the Senate, the bookseller who had his shop opposite our apartment emerged from the post office, looked over my shoulder and said in surprise, 'But what's all this?'

Straggling across the road to join me were the people who'd signed up for my second tour – all twenty-seven of them.

I shrugged. '*Mes admirateurs.*'

'*Merde alors,*' he said respectfully.

I've lost count of the people I've shown around literary Paris since. Hundreds, certainly – and, through books I've written, many hundreds of thousands. But, in explaining the city to them, it has taught me much more. And yet there is always more to learn.

Many people who visit Paris will return home with nothing but sore feet and an Eiffel Tower paperweight. The lucky ones will have experienced at least a glimpse and a taste of this most fascinating and intricate of cities. Enough, at least, to be able to say, in that most evocatively nostalgic of phrases 'I remember ... once ... in Paris.'

I hope this book helps.

ART AND CULTURE

CAFÉS AND LITERATURE

During the 1950s, when Jean-Paul Sartre and Simone de Beauvoir lived at the Hôtel La Louisiane – in separate rooms, to accommodate their other 'contingent' relationships – the Café de Flore was their home-from-home. 'We installed ourselves completely,' Sartre explained. 'From nine to twelve a.m., we worked. Then we had lunch, and at two p.m. we came back and spoke with friends we had met, until eight p.m.. After having dinner, we received people with whom we had fixed an appointment. This could seem strange to you, but at this café, we were at home.'

Despite this endorsement, Canadian writer Mavis Gallant, a long-time Paris expatriate, dismissed cafés as venues for literary creation. 'The other day,' she wrote, 'I was asked, in all seriousness, where one can see authors at work in cafés. It sounded for all the world like watching chimpanzees riding tricycles: both are unnatural occupations. I have only one friend who still writes her novels in notebooks, in cafés. She chooses cafés that are ordinary and charmless … If anyone she knows discovers the café, she changes at once for another, more obscure, hard to get to. About café writing, in general, old legends and ancient myths die hard.'

Some writers in the past did work in cafés, but only because they had nowhere else. Rooms without heating or sanitation did nothing to inspire creativity. James Baldwin wrote most of his first novel in Le Select, the one café in Montparnasse designated to stay open all night. A few decades earlier, it provided a haven for the poet Hart Crane and his fellow alcoholics, joined by prostitutes, and the friendless and sleepless of Paris's bohemia.

Ernest Hemingway hadn't been in Paris very long before he discovered that a two-room apartment shared with his wife, Hadley, and baby was no place to create. When Gertrude Stein visited to read some of his stories, the only place she could do so was seated on the bed in the bedroom while they waited outside. Thereafter, he was seldom home. Each day, he worked in a corner of the Closerie des Lilas and, after returning home to share dinner with Hadley, left her literally holding the baby to write for a few more hours in a rented room around the corner.

The alpha male of the Montparnasse expatriate community, he regarded the Closerie as his territory, and defended it aggressively. In *A Moveable Feast* (1964) he describes just starting to write when someone says 'Hi, Hem. What are you trying to do? Write in a café?' Your luck has run out and you shut the notebook. This was the worst thing that could happen. Now, you could get out and hope it was an accidental visit and that the visitor had only come in by chance and there was not going to be an infestation. It was probably wiser to move but the anger started to come and I said, 'Listen. A bitch like you has plenty of places to go. Why do you have to come here and louse a decent café?'

Other creative people also congregated in cafés, but they weren't writers and, rather than working, they were looking for work. With private telephones almost unknown, musicians, bit-part actors, artists' models, prostitutes and anyone else who relied on casual employment gathered in specific cafés where potential employers knew to find them. They spent the day reading, playing cards or chess, and waiting for a job. Musicians carried something that signified their instrument: a violin bow or a clarinet reed tucked into their hatband. Some actors wore costumes and make-up, ready to go to work.

All this changed in the 1950s, when cafés discovered there was more money in meals than beverages. These days, it's only in coffee shop chains that one can occupy a table for the entire day. Managers grit their teeth as clients plug in their laptop the moment the doors open and remain there, hogging a table and barely covering the cost of electricity with the occasional *latte*. Some may be working on the Great American Novel but most are just surfing the net. As for anyone writing by hand in a café, they are generally a student composing a postcard to the folks back home, probably beginning, 'You won't believe where I'm writing this.' Whatever their activities, café writers these days are almost invariably foreign. A French writer is as likely to work in a café as a French dentist. For the French, writing is not a trade but a calling, and should be conducted with appropriate gravity – and in private.

BUSKERS, BEGGARS AND MIMES

Parisian beggars don't beg. Some kneel. Others sit, legs drawn up, heads bowed on knees, eyes downcast, with '*1 euro pour manger*' (1 euro to eat) lettered on a card or chalked on the sidewalk. Some have a dog for company or, very occasionally, a child. Silence and stillness make them seem more noble than pathetic; living statues, eloquent of suffering. Their saucers or paper cups contain only centimes. Larger coins go straight in their pockets, rather than ruin the effect of penniless misery.

It's in the nature of the French to see charity in practical rather than moral terms. Virtue as an abstraction is viewed sceptically. The French rationale for giving money to a beggar runs something like the following. A beggar is not demanding money for nothing. He's selling something: a sense of having done a good deed; a feeling of generosity, of virtue. So in a way he's a small businessman. You should treat him the same as if he sold newspapers or cigarettes. You just need to ask yourself, 'Do I need a beggar today?'

It's difficult to make a similar case for buskers. Street musicians serve no social purpose. Nor are their performances particularly accomplished – except when, on rare occasions, the challenges of singing at the top of one's voice in all weathers encourage rather than extinguish an exceptional talent. Édith Piaf was such an artist. She became a singer to attract spectators for her father, a street acrobat and contortionist. A club owner took her off the streets, taught her to discipline her voice, coaxed her into her trademark little black dress, and made her famous. It was entirely consistent with the rules of this hardest of hard schools that, when he refused to sell her contract to some old friends from her street-singing days, he was murdered, possibly with her connivance. '*Je ne regrette rien*,' she sang defiantly. I regret nothing.

Britain's Henry VIII swore to 'whip unlicensed minstrels and players, fortune-tellers, pardoners and fencers, as well as beggars'. Conditions for buskers haven't improved markedly since, least of all in Paris, where street performers risk being hassled and robbed by rivals, mocked and abused by drunken football fans, and arrested by the *gendarmerie* for creating a public nuisance.

The city introduced assigned locations and legal busking in 1989, after teams of musicians brawled over the best pitches, notably weekend cinema queues. RATP, the authority for the Métro, instituted a similar system. Buskers must now audition before a panel of assessors chosen from RATP employees. If they pass, they're given an official permit and a location in which to perform. Those who try to cheat can be fined and risk having their instruments confiscated.

The luxury of official approval encouraged some to lift their game. One still sees the lone accordion or clarinet player, and the occasional young man with a guitar, a harmonica frame bent from a coat hanger and a repertoire of old Bob Dylan songs. But it's more usual for the Métro to boom with Peruvian octets in ponchos playing panpipes, bulbous guitars and drums. Small string orchestras are not unknown, nor jazz groups which, scorning 'When the Saints Go Marching In', offer bop standards like 'Well, You Needn't'.

Unlicensed performers keep to the shadows. Some congregate on the platforms at Châtelet, the largest and most complex of the multi-route interchanges. Alert always for the travel police, they step into a carriage and start playing before the doors have even closed, aiming to complete a verse or two and pass the hat before the next station, where they alight and, crossing to the opposite platform, find a new audience going in the other direction.

Away from the tourist-rich central arrondissements, illegals are more common and, correspondingly, inventive. On Line 2 (Porte Dauphine–Nation) a man and girl – father and daughter? – stretch a curtain between two uprights to create a makeshift stage and present a quick Punch-and-Judy sketch about the president's love life. They're followed by an unconvincingly well-fed West Indian who drones through a prepared speech outlining his need for a square meal.

His performance, worn smooth from repetition, makes all the more startling the abrupt appearance of a young man in shirt-sleeves whose bare feet appear twisted by some deformity so that he waddles, bow-legged, all his weight on his ankles. Muttering an incomprehensible spiel, he sidles and elbows his way through the embarrassed passengers, outsize trousers dragging on the dusty floor, open palm waggling under their noses. A few part with a coin and avert their eyes from his affliction until the train arrives at the next station – 'Place Blanche' murmurs a voice over the public address system – and he darts onto the platform … where his feet, miraculously, return to normal, and a pair of moccasins materialize from the pockets of his trousers – which, hitched up now and the belt tightened, fit perfectly. Coins jingling in his pocket, he slips, grinning, into the crowd.

In the 1970s, it was rare, particularly in central Paris on the weekend, not to encounter a mime. Often in troupes, they were particularly numerous on the sloping Place de l'Horloge in front of the Centre Pompidou where crowds waiting to enter art exhibitions offered a captive audience. Many were young Americans, drawn by the celebrity of Marcel Marceau and Bip, his chalk-faced alter ego with the comic top hat and flower. Among those doggedly climbing imaginary stairs and struggling to escape from non-existent glass boxes was future Hollywood star Jessica Lange. She may even have participated in a group mime popular at the time. In a variation on another cliché of the form, the slow-motion walk, performers, sometimes singly, sometimes in pairs, pretended to battle an illusory gale. Dressed uniformly in jumpsuits of metallized fabric, they struggled, head-down and bent almost double, to forge into a non-existent hurricane, slogging a few painful steps, only to be driven inexorably backwards.

Except for an occasional human statue, mimes are rare today. An exception came in 2012. At the behest of the *mairie* (municipal hall), squads known as Pierrots de la Nuit were sent out in an effort to reduce the city's nocturnal noise pollution. Did they approach noisy mobs of drunken British football fans, making 'sshh, sshh' gestures and putting fingers to lips? If so, it's not surprising that nothing was heard from them again.

JEAN-LUC GODARD AND LA NOUVELLE VAGUE

T he death in 2022 of Jean-Luc Godard called 'Cut' on the movement known as the *nouvelle vague* (the New Wave). Its other founding members, François Truffaut, Claude Chabrol, Éric Rohmer and Jacques Rivette, pre-deceased him, leaving him sole spokesperson for the radical rethink of cinema they pioneered.

Not that they had much in common, either as artists or men. Truffaut, a school drop-out, juvenile delinquent and army deserter, looked to be headed for a life of crime, just as certainly as genial, pipe-smoking Claude Chabrol seemed destined to follow his parents and become a suburban pharmacist. Rivette was reclusive, a solitary intellectual. 'Nothing but making films interested him,' said a mourner at his funeral. Godard was the true wild card. Son of a wealthy Swiss doctor, well-read, multi-lingual, with a quicksilver mind and wit, he appeared the worst-suited of any of them to the perceived superficiality of cinema.

But all were transformed by their encounter with Henri Langlois, Director of the national film museum, the Cinémathèque Française in Paris. An improbable ideologue, overweight, untidy and unkempt, he seduced them with his vision of film as a landscape of almost infinite variety, in contrast to the films produced under the political and aesthetic paralysis of de Gaulle's Fourth Republic. Disgusted by plodding plot-obsessed melodramas, Truffaut, in one of his incendiary essays, dismissed them as a *cinema de papa* (Daddy's films).

His impatience coincided with developments in the technique of cinema; lightweight cameras, sensitive microphones, fast stock that needed less light. In 1948, director Alexandre Astruc theorized about the *caméra-stylo*, an instrument with which a 'filmmaker/author could write with his camera as a writer writes with his pen'. In 1960, it began to seem a possibility. For the first time, French directors could aspire to the qualities Truffaut defined as the virtues of low-budget American cinema – 'grace, lightness, modesty, elegance and speed'.

With no jobs going in movies, Godard went to work as a publicist for an American distribution company, writing biographical pieces about Hollywood actors and actresses. 'I didn't know anything about these people,' he confessed, 'so I just made them up. They were my first movies.' He dedicated his first feature, *À bout de souffle* (Breathless) to Monogram Pictures, cheapest studio on Hollywood's 'Poverty Row'. His spasmodic cutting and the airily casual camerawork of Raoul Coutard overturned conceptions of the well-made film, and made stars of both leading actor Jean-Paul Belmondo and Godard himself, who 'tore up the rule book', observed a critic, 'but didn't bother to read it first'.

Almost everyone got Godard wrong – the effect for which he strove. British critic Kenneth Tynan was one of the few to see through his pose. 'The image I get from his films,' he wrote, 'is that of a young man in a trench coat with his hands in his pockets; a cigarette droops from one corner of his mouth as he talks in snatches, plentifully interrupted with shrugs, out of the other. He speaks softly and swiftly, in an undertone made eloquent by deadpan wit, superbly timed pauses, audacious changes of tempo and persistent narrative zest: we recognize the born spell-binder who does not need to raise his voice.'

Godard wasn't the trench coat type, but in every other respect Tynan was right. He did indeed speak softly and swiftly, in both French and English. And if he did hesitate, it was as characters do in a Harold Pinter play – to let silence speak for itself. Among *cinéastes* (those knowledgeable

about the cinema) and, increasingly, the chattering classes, his *aperçus* became famous, passed around like bonbons: 'Photography is the truth – so cinema is the truth twenty-four times a second'; 'A story should have a beginning, a middle and an end – just not necessarily in that order.' And his generation were 'the children of Marx and Coca-Cola', while he was '*Marxiste – tendance Groucho*'.

He was above all a director of women. *Le Mepris* (Contempt) transformed Brigitte Bardot's trashy image, and he turned Anna Karina, his first wife, into what *Cahiers du Cinéma* in its heyday would have called 'an axiom of the screen'. The shot from *Alphaville* of her standing at a window with a copy of poet Paul Éluard's collection *Capitale de la douleur* (Capital of Pain) recalled Josef von Sternberg's direction to Marlene Dietrich on *Morocco*: 'Count to six, then look at that light as if you can't live without it.'

His work tailed off as his health declined, but occasionally one saw flashes of the old Godard. Presented in 1998 with an honorary César, France's equivalent of an Oscar, he wandered on stage at the glitzy presentation ceremony that took place at the Théâtre des Champs-Élysées in Paris, looking, as usual, as if he'd just got out of bed and dressed in the dark. From one jacket pocket dangled a bedraggled scarf that dragged behind him. Unnoticed by him? Or, rather, artfully placed so as to trail across the stage?

Few sites in Paris are specifically associated with Godard or the *nouvelle vague* in general. The doors of the original Cinémathèque, under the Palais de Chaillot at Trocadero, have a superstitious significance for any *cinéaste*, and figure in a number of their films, while photographs of Jean-Pierre Léaud, Truffaut's *comedian fetish*, haranguing the ranks of anonymous CRS men as they prepare to charge, has become part of the 1968 legend. On Boulevard Raspail, near the intersection with Boulevard Edgar Quinet, a well-meaning but poorly informed council has designated a spot as the place where Belmondo met his end in *À bout de souffle*, a demise that actually happened across the road in rue Campagne Première. But to his admirers, Godard is everywhere. Look at a stretch of freeway along the Seine near the Gare d'Austerlitz and you will see Eddie Constantine as Lemmy Caution, tough-guy hero of American pulp fiction, setting off through sidereal space in a Cadillac convertible en route to the futuristic city of Alphaville and his encounter with Karina's Natacha von Braun. As is chiselled on the tomb of Christopher Wren, designer of London's St Paul's Cathedral, '*Si monumentum requiris, circumspice*' (If you seek his monument, look around).

ART NOUVEAU

The apartment building at 29 Avenue Rapp, in the 7th arrondissement, doesn't immediately invite the label 'Home, Sweet Home'. Vines sculpted in stone crawl and writhe up the first two floors, entwining the relief of a nude Eve who lounges enticingly on one side of the front windows while, on the other, Adam squirms in his genital fig leaf. Between them, a bust of the architect's wife looks out reprovingly from above an entrance whose ovoid windows and elongated front door give an initial impression of bulbous slanted eyes but, on closer inspection, represent a pair of testicles and a lengthy penis. Bronze door handles shaped like lizards (slang in France for penis) add a further disturbing touch.

Above the first two floors, the design becomes less extravagant, even paying lip service to Haussmann's concept of the ideal building: six storeys high, with long balconies at the second and fifth floors – except that the top balcony is a faux-Venetian colonnade decorated with coloured tiles, produced, like those that cover the frontage above, by Alexander Bigot, who pioneered the high-fired polychrome ceramics which gave many of Paris's Art Nouveau buildings a vitreous gleam. His inventive use of colour suggests the tiled interiors and ironwork of Moorish Spain and in particular Granada's Alhambra. Bigot was a friend and collaborator of the building's architect, Jules Lavirotte, who took advantage of his expertise to add his signature in Art Nouveau lettering on a ceramic panel embedded in the façade.

If, as many commentators during the *belle époque* suggested, France was the woman of Europe and Paris, therefore, the woman of France, it was fitting that the city should have welcomed an artistic movement which embodied the feminine principle: Art Nouveau. A voluptuous style that appeared in the late nineteenth century and flourished until the First World War, it found inspiration in the natural world. Wrought iron was drawn out into sinuously curved, vine-like staircases, tinted glass and bronzed metal combined in lamps and windows that recalled the wings of insects, while every detail hinted at the curve of a hip, the droop of a breast, the tumble of a woman's hair.

Although it was taken up in France and, particularly, in Belgium, where the best surviving examples are found, Art Nouveau was not a French creation. Rather, it spilled over from the rich goulash of Jewish, Catholic and

Teutonic influences that simmered in the cauldron of the Austro-Hungarian Empire. The man who did most to introduce it to France, Alphonse Mucha, arrived from Moravia (part of modern day Czech Republic) in 1888. Within a decade he had become famous for his posters, which combined influences from numerous cultures: the gold of Russian icons and the inexpressive stare of their virgins and saints; the gilt, enamel and lacquered wood of bourgeois Vienna; the eroticism of Budapest, with its links to Asia; the middle-European Roma culture, the women of which provided the period's most sensual models and courtesans.

Architects like Lavirotte, ceramicist Bigot, metal forger Edgar Brandt, and Hector Guimard, who designed the entrances to the Paris Métro, were typical of artists who abandoned the plain and symmetrical Haussmann style for something more irregular and exotic. In Nancy, glassmaker Émile Gallé used layers of molten *pâte de verre* to create objects that looked eerily organic, while in the United States Louis Comfort Tiffany's lamps of coloured glass mounted in bronze are classics of their kind.

Ironworker Louis Majorelle, introduced to Art Nouveau by Gallé, adapted the style to both metal and wood. His furniture, decorated in marquetry, with inlaid images in coloured wood, have few rivals, while his sinuous, entwining balconies and banisters of painted, gilded wrought iron and brass for the Galeries Lafayette department store in Paris are one of the glories of the style.

Among the more unexpected artists to employ Art Nouveau was American dancer Loïe Fuller. Enveloping her body in layers of painted silk gauze onto which coloured glass slides were projected, she extended the length of her arms with rods and, whirling, turned herself into a *tourbillion* (whirlwind) of colour and light. Architect Henri Sauvage designed the theatre for her performances at the 1900 Paris Exposition, the interior of which by Francis Jourdain won a gold medal. Sculptors, in particular François-Raoul Larche, recreated her in bronze, the embodiment of Art Nouveau's feminine inspiration.

Towards the end of the nineteenth century, the Paris city authorities encouraged any architecture that broke with the Haussmannian model, then considered old-fashioned. As a result, Lavirotte's Art Nouveau buildings were initially acclaimed, winning prizes between 1901 and 1904 for the most original new façades. But his popularity waned with the novelty of the new style, and he found that clients, while still wanting a touch of Art Nouveau, preferred something more staid. His private life also affected his work. His nouveau riche Burgundian family, who never accepted his choice of career, objected violently to him marrying the divorced and six years older Jane de Montchenu, wife of his art school professor. These tensions exacerbated a volatile mental state, and he spent much of his later life in institutions, in one of which he died in 1929.

By 1910, Art Nouveau was no longer *nouveau*. It survived until the First World War, but post-war German design brought the Bauhaus, which championed a simpler, smoother, streamlined taste, a tendency Paris began to see in the less florid architecture, sharper edges and clearer lines of Art Moderne, later to be rechristened Art Deco.

WHO WAS THAT MASKED MAN?
THE OPÉRA AND ITS PHANTOM

In an anecdote so famous it's almost certainly false, the Empress Eugénie, consort of Napoleon III, viewed with confusion the new Opera House commissioned by her husband from a design by young architect Charles Garnier. Contemplating its colonnaded façade, gilded angels, rearing winged horses and statuary groups, including Carpeaux's *La Danse*, showing the god Bacchus surrounded by nude bacchantes (which one irate citizen had already judged obscene and pelted with ink), she enquired, 'It's spectacular, M. Garnier but ... it's not Renaissance, not Baroque, not Classical. What style is it?'

Garnier responded with the answer for which generations of architects, faced with touchy clients, have blessed his name.

'Why, your imperial highness,' he said, 'it's *your* style!'

In 1875, the Nouvel Opéra de Paris was the last word in construction. Its presence made this, almost overnight, the most fashionable district of Paris. The district oozed innovation. The world's first public presentation of motion pictures by the Lumière brothers took place in December 1895 at Le Salon Indien in the basement of the Grand Café on Boulevard des Capucines. Department stores such as Galeries Lafayette and Au Printemps seized whole blocks of nearby boulevards, using the swirls and curlicues of Art Nouveau to create temples to commerce. Galeries

Lafayette's domed roof of glass and iron alone was an architectural wonder, so strong that the store offered 25,000 francs to the first aircraft to land on it. They took the roof down during the First World War, for fear it might be smashed by German bombing or artillery, but once it was reassembled Jules Védrines succeeded on 19 January 1919, at the cost of wrecking his plane and injuring himself. A monument on the roof marks the spot.

The Hotel de la Paix, opposite the Opéra, became the preferred playground of army officers and their *cocottes*, who gathered in its suites for champagne, morphine and sex. Émile Zola's anti-heroine Nana expires there of smallpox. More exclusive still, on nearby Place Vendôme, former waiter César Ritz and *chef de cuisine* Georges Auguste Escoffier launched the Hôtel Ritz with staff and supplies looted from London's Savoy, where both previously worked. Paradoxically, however, Garnier's building would become world famous not for the wealth it created nor the works performed on its stage, but rather for a trashy novel that exploited its name.

In 1871, the anarchist uprising known as the Paris Commune convulsed Paris. In its aftermath, hundreds were executed without trial, others deported, and many jailed. The police, overwhelmed with the volume of prisoners, held some in cellars under the Opéra site. Among the journalists covering their subsequent trial was Gaston Leroux. Already a successful author of crime stories, he saw the dramatic possibilities of a mystery set in the building, but, more importantly, beneath it.

Garnier, realizing that the water table under his site was only a few metres below the surface, had laid a concrete 'raft', or caisson, to block any water welling up from below. Throughout the thirteen years it took to complete construction, steam pumps operated around the clock to keep the foundations dry. This detail gave Leroux the image of a cloaked and masked figure propelling himself across a dark subterranean lake. With its addition, pulp was transformed into a classic.

The Phantom of the Opera appeared as a newspaper serial in 1909 and 1910, and in English the following year. Leroux didn't let reality limit his imagination. He'd read that a stagehand died when a curtain counterweight fell on him. Might this have been no accident, but murder? And what if it wasn't a weight that fell but the giant chandelier that hung in the central cupola over the heads of an unsuspecting audience? As to who might have committed these crimes, Leroux pirated the plot of *Beauty and the Beast*, and reached back to such Gothic novels of the previous century as *The Castle of Otranto* and *The Mysteries of Udolpho*, in which helpless females

were imprisoned under apparently haunted castles. Out of these emerged the story of the disfigured Erik who, having been in construction before his accident, knew the Opéra well enough to secretly move around and under it, materializing backstage, in dressing rooms and private boxes; even appearing in costume as Edgar Allen Poe's Red Death at a masked ball. He befriends a young soprano, Christine Daaé, coaches her, and sabotages a star so that she can sing in her place, all the while remaining invisible. When Christine's lover makes an appearance, the stage is set for a grand *dénouement* in which Erik takes her to his lair and reveals his ravaged face.

Most audiences outside France discovered Leroux's story through the 1925 film starring Lon Chaney, who screwed metal rings into his eye sockets to create a spectral stare and wired back his nose to suggest a skull from which the flesh had been burned. The moment where Mary Philbin whips off Chaney's mask became a milestone in cinema melodrama.

So vivid was the impression created by Chaney, of Erik transporting Christine beneath the Opéra, that the existence of the lake was assumed. Water did enter the foundations once the pumps were turned off, but only in one space, and then to the depth of about a metre, shallow enough for a man to stand upright. According to the Opéra's current historian, Pierre Vidal, 'the pressure of the water in the tank stops any more rising up through the foundations, and the weight of the tank stabilizes the building'. Today, this cistern, inaccessible except through a grating, is visited only by firefighters to practise using underwater breathing apparatus in the dark. The only permanent residents are catfish, blind and white.

Not that the Opéra is without phantoms. In 1991, the LVMH (Louis Vuitton) Foundation financed the restoration of an archive and library in the wing where Napoleon and Eugénie once entertained at post-performance suppers. For the gala unveiling, imperial guardsmen in silver breastplates lined the grand staircase, while, at the first landing, Culture Minister Jack Lang and historian Emmanuel Le Roy Ladurie waited to welcome guests.

In the main foyer, as the glitterati sipped champagne, a figure appeared at the edge of the crowd. A true spectre at the feast, his ragged appearance mocked the formal gowns and evening dress. A beret barely covered a near-hairless head, and a loose sweater and baggy cords hung on his emaciated body. Many saw him but, as when Erik appeared as the Red Death, none acknowledged his presence. Finally he spotted some friendly faces and dived into the crowd, which parted silently and closed after him. Rudolf Nureyev, former Director of the Paris Opéra Ballet, was dying of Aids, and had little more than a year to live, but to those who had once cheered him on the stage of this building, he was already dead.

JOHNNY

NO DIRECTION HOME

One expects artists of note – Picasso, Rembrandt, Dalí – to be known by their surnames. Politicians too – Mitterrand, Churchill, Trump. Some writers also rate the honour – Hemingway, Shakespeare, Salinger. But how many personalities are identified by their Christian names alone?

Well, there's Elvis, and Orson, and maybe Adele – and, in France, another rare example. No French person will wonder whom you mean if you ask what they think of 'Johnny'.

Singer and actor Jean-Philippe Léo Smet, alias Johnny Hallyday, was a phenomenon – but only in France. He sold more than 110 million records, among them five diamond albums, twenty-two platinum and forty gold – but all in France. He also appeared in fifty movies – almost all made in France – and repeatedly sold out concerts before hundreds of thousands of people, which were then watched by millions more on television – but only in France. As a (British) obituary put it, 'It would be difficult to exaggerate the place Hallyday occupied in the collective memory and hearts of his countrymen. Outside France, with the honourable exceptions of French-speaking Belgium and Switzerland, he was viewed mostly with bemusement.'

If someone was to introduce France to a post-war world dominated by American pop, Johnny was your man. Rugged, handsome, aggressively heterosexual, he was an outsized and noisy cuckoo in the cosy nest of French popular music. His competitors were folksy *chansonniers* (cabaret-style performers) like George Brassens and Jacques Brel, descendants of Charles Trenet who sang about clouds, flowers and the girls of yesteryear, or such balladeers as Charles Aznavour, complaining of loneliness and lost love. Any balls in the business belonged to the late Édith Piaf, who, a generation earlier, would have taken Hallyday to bed. He was just her type.

Foreign critics accused Johnny of imitating Elvis Presley – but he imitated everybody. More than a quarter of his recordings were covers of American hits. His breakout hit was 'Let's Twist Again' – sung in English. In 1967, at the height of Flower Power, he recorded Scott McKenzie's 'San Francisco (Be Sure to Wear Flowers in Your Hair)'. After watching him sing it on television, wearing silver lamé trousers, white shoes, beads, a velvet jacket with floral motifs, and carrying a rose, one French critic commented sourly, 'Johnny poses with a lost, dreamy gaze, tending towards a beaten dog.'

All that changed when he discovered his forte, the staged concert, and his image, a synthesis of Clint Eastwood, Elvis Presley and the Marlon Brando of *The Wild One*, leather-clad leader of the Black Rebels Motor Cycle Club. 'Whatcha rebelling against, Johnny?', someone asks. Brando, with a sneer, responds 'Whatcha got?'

Stylists worked to maximize Johnny's physical presence – the stertorous baritone, the leonine glare, the mane-like quiff – and put him in what became his standard wardrobe, a distillation of Biker Chic: blue cotton vest, often sweat-soaked; snug jeans; biker boots; and a leather belt, heavily buckled. Jewellery tended to knuckle-duster rings, silver skull pendants and chains.

Titanic quantities of machinery and a team of hundreds lay behind his stage manner of arrogance and isolation. In 1998, just after France won the World Cup, Hallyday filled the vast 80,000-seat Stade de France. A helicopter lowered him by cable to its roof, from where he descended, in a cloud of smoke and fireworks, to a stage afloat in an ocean of ecstatic fans. Expressionless, he surveyed them, removed his dark glasses, and tossed them into the mob. *Que la fête commence!* His millennium show at the Eiffel Tower outdid even this; a million people attended, and ten million watched on television.

After Charles de Gaulle snorted that all this frenzy suggested the youth of France had too much excess energy, and might do better if drafted into road gangs, Johnny made it his business to cultivate friendships in high places. He got on with Jacques Chirac, who liked to present himself as working class, and was even closer to Nicolas Sarkozy. The latter officiated at one of his weddings. Chirac awarded him the Légion d'honneur.

Not overly creative – he confessed to only writing a couple of songs, and those while high on cocaine – Johnny kept close to the limelight, but always slightly out of its glare. Rather than make physical contact with the crowd, he entered from above or from darkness. Sometimes he rode his Harley on stage and remained straddling it while he sang. Rather than mingle, he utilized a silent team of bodyguards that materialized out of the dark. Ringed by them, Johnny made a deliberate, menacing progress through the human ocean, alone in an island of space.

He was careful to maintain his American credentials, living part-time in Los Angeles (although legally in Switzerland, a fact that led to accusations of tax irregularities), partying with the Rolling Stones and Jimi Hendrix, but periodically riding his Harley into the Nevada desert, where, if his publicists could be believed, he enjoyed staying in small motels, incognito – but never, cynics noted, without a video crew close at hand. Despite five marriages and numerous liaisons, he never put down any roots. That was part of his image. Just a drifter. Just passing through. Moving on. Still French. Still Johnny.

Since September 2021, he has had a monument in Paris. The forecourt before the arena in Bercy (in the 12th arrondissement), where he appeared in more than one hundred concerts, became Esplanade Johnny Hallyday, with a creation by Bertrand Lavier entitled '*Quelque chose de ...*' (Something about ...). High overhead, a real Harley-Davidson perches on a column in the form of

a guitar neck. The title refers to '*Quelque chose de Tennessee*', a 1985 hit inspired by playwright Tennessee Williams. A video clip produced for the song shows Johnny, ever the loner, driving a truck and hitchhiking across a monochrome American Midwest. Reverently, Johnny's mistress at the time of his death in 2017, actress Nathalie Baye, reads a quote from Williams' *Cat on a Hot Tin Roof*: 'Oh, you weak, beautiful people who give up with such grace. What you need is someone to take hold of you – gently, with love, and hand your life back to you, ...' Ah, Johnny. If it wasn't for the cocaine, the tax evasion and the girls, you could almost qualify for saint.

IF I CAN MAKE IT THERE
ART IN THE AIR

T hanks to a franc devalued by the First World War, money went further in Paris than in any city in Europe. Ernest Hemingway gloated in 1921 that one could live there for a year on $1,000, and Scott Fitzgerald marvelled that a four-course meal, with wine, was available for the equivalent of 18 cents. Every ambitious artist or writer headed for Paris, convinced that 'in the city of boulevard bars and Baudelaire', as Alice Toklas put it, art was 'a contagious craft', to be contracted like a virus by simply breathing air thick with tobacco, drinking unlimited red wine, and, above all, hanging out at the Rotonde or Café du Dôme.

Although a few local painters, among them Jules Pascin, Tsuguharu Foujita, Chaïm Soutine and Kees van Dongen, became the nucleus of a School of Paris, serious artists in Montparnasse were soon outnumbered by students and hobby painters, writers and musicians, frequently foreign, and a floating population of loafers and drifters.

For centuries, the serious study of art, aside from the ateliers of various artists and a few private schools such as Académie Julian, took place at the École des Beaux-Arts. Candidates for its four-year course had first to demonstrate superior talent. Once admitted and having paid its substantial fees, they were hit with an additional weekly charge, known as *le masse*, to cover models, lighting, cleaning, soap, towels and turpentine.

Within the school, a pecking order prevailed. In life classes, seniors monopolized the front seats. Freshmen – the Beaux-Arts didn't admit women – were also expected to run errands for the seniors and clean their studios.

The curriculum overwhelmingly favoured tradition and the classics. Students spent their first year drawing from plaster casts of Greek and Roman sculpture. Life classes used professional models who had mastered a repertoire of poses based on the same statuary and refused indignantly to vary them. French students persevered, since a diploma was essential for professional success. By 1900, however, a third of the Beaux-Arts students were foreigners, many of them Americans who, increasingly impatient with its methods, looked towards Montparnasse and its independent art schools: the Académie de la Grande Chaumière, the Académie Carmen and, in particular, the Académie Colarossi, started in 1870 by sculptor Filippo Colarossi.

One Beaux-Arts professor dismissed the new schools as 'a ramshackle set of studios where artists and students could pay to use the models and receive a little tutoring if they wished', but both students and instructors found their freedom exhilarating. Artists who studied or taught at Colarossi's include Paul Gauguin, sculptor Camille Claudel and couturier Paul Poiret. Some teachers were expatriates themselves, notably the German-American Lyonel Feininger and German George Grosz. Alphonse Mucha, Czech master of the swirling Art Nouveau style, anathema to the Beaux-Arts, taught a popular course at Colarossi's, which in 1911 appointed its first female teacher, and an expatriate as well, New Zealand artist Frances Hodgkins.

Colarossi's and Académie de la Grande Chaumière charged fees only for their morning sculpture courses, taught by such established figures as Ossip Zadkine and Antoine Bourdelle. Those attending afternoon and evening sketching classes could pay by the session: as little as 50 centimes; less than a horse-bus ride. Women were welcome, nor was there an entry requirement. Sunday painters from the suburbs could find themselves drawing the same model as Amedeo Modigliani, who, habitually broke, was a regular at Colarossi's when not in the Rotonde, sketching portraits for drinking money.

Other innovations included evening sessions under electric light, though the atmosphere at these was oppressive. 'All the rooms were packed,' complained Russian painter Marevna (Marie Vorobiev). 'In the one where we were drawing from the nude, the air was stifling because of an overheated stove. We were positively melting in an inferno permeated by the strong

smell of perspiring bodies mixed with scent, fresh paint, damp waterproofs and dirty feet; all this was intensified by the thick smoke from cigarettes and the strong tobacco of pipe smokers.'

Female students faced other shocks. Scots artist Kathleen Bruce described her first day at Colarossi's in 1901: 'At the end of the studio passed, one by one, a string of nude male models. Each jumped for a moment on to the model throne, took a pose and jumped down. The model for the day was being chosen. Before reason could control instinct, I turned and fled, shut myself in the lavatory, and was sick.'

Few of the artist emigrants stayed long. As money or confidence ran out, they returned home, where the experience of Paris might win them jobs as teachers, illustrators or designers for the theatre or films. They carried with them the myth of Montparnasse and its cafés as the ultimate artists' playground. As one giddy visitor murmured in 1929, 'My dear, at first I was uncertain whether the Dôme was a place or a state of mind or a disease. It is all three!'

LE JAZZ
HOT OR NOT?

The exact definition and origin of 'jazz' is still debated. Emerging as 'jass' in the American South during the late nineteenth century as a synonym for sex, the word became attached to any music played where that commodity was sold, notably the 'sporting houses' of New Orleans' brothel quarter, Storyville. After F. Scott Fitzgerald declared the 1920s to be the Jazz Age, it came to mean the act of enlivening the prosaic with provocative modernity. Any dance, dress or design could be 'jazzed up' with a little creative dissonance.

White audiences preferred 'race music', as recording companies then called it, to appear wholly 'natural' and spontaneous, trailing a whiff of the primitive. Harlem's Cotton Club advertised sophisticated composer/arranger Duke Ellington as the leading exponent of 'jungle music', while, for a 1932 movie short, America's most gifted jazz trumpeter, Louis Armstrong, was cajoled into a leopard skin.

Before the First World War, minstrel singers, sand-dancers, cake-walkers and comics in blackface touring under the 'jazz' banner imported the music into Europe. But jazz only caught on in France with the arrival in 1917 of a sixty-person all-African-American Marine Corps troupe to entertain the troops and accustom the French to the presence of foreigners on their soil. Its director, James Reese Europe, formerly led the orchestra for dance duo Vernon and Irene Castle. His sidemen were all accomplished sight readers but, respecting the prevailing prejudices, memorized their scores and performed them without sheet music. This reinforced the idea that playing jazz was a skill unique to African-Americans, and French entrepreneurs began importing them to play it. Such shows as Lew Leslie's *Blackbirds* (1928) were an instant success. Even when the French government bowed to union pressure and required that three local musicians be employed for each foreigner, it was cheaper for producers to pay dozens of French musicians to sit backstage, silent, as Americans performed.

Dancers in Europe's troupe, including the famous Bill 'Bojangles' Robinson, were no less innovative, introducing steps unknown to French artists trained in the classical repertoire. Erik Satie incorporated the most popular of them, the one-step, into his 1917 ballet *Parade*, which, danced by Léonide Massine, caused a sensation. 'For the first time, music hall was invading Art-with-a-capital-A!' wrote young composer Francis Poulenc, who attended the premiere. 'A one-step danced in *Parade*! When that began, the audience let loose with boos and applause.' After the premiere, enraged dowagers advanced on librettist Jean Cocteau with needle-sharp hatpins. Fortunately, the poet Guillaume Apollinaire was in the audience, in uniform and recuperating from a war wound, representing all the men who were fighting for France. 'If it had not been for Apollinaire in uniform,' Cocteau wrote, 'with his skull shaved, the scar on his temple and the bandage around his head, the women would have gouged our eyes out.'

During the 1920s, every boat from New York brought a new dance craze, as well as a fresh African-American ensemble to demonstrate it. Parisians learned the foxtrot, renamed *le fox*, as well as the shimmy, tango, rhumba and Charleston. Since a new dance seldom lasted more than a season, everyone rushed to cash in. When Gilda Gray popularized the shimmy, couturiers created dresses with layers of fringe that fanned out as the dancer shook her shoulders and breasts. Meanwhile, scouts for the Folies Bergère combed dance schools for an American to train as their own shimmy star. One they considered was an amateur who, at twenty-eight, was a little old for a stage début, but she wasn't interested anyway, so they crossed Zelda Fitzgerald off their list, leaving her to pursue her doomed attempt at a ballet career.

Young composers of the avant-garde, particularly those from the group known as Les Six, experimented with the folk music of other countries, hoping to find an equivalent to jazz. Visiting Brazil, Darius Milhaud adapted a popular song, 'O Boi no Telhado' (The Ox on the Roof), into a ballet for Cocteau, who also opened a Paris cabaret of the same name. Poulenc made his composing début in 1917 with '*Rapsodie nègre*' for a baritone and a chamber group. Its nonsense texts, including such lines as '*Pata ta bo banana loumandes/ Golas Glebes ikrous/ Banana lou ito kous kous/ pota la ma Honoloulou*,' were supposedly by Makoko Kangourou, a poet from Liberia, the African state created as a haven for freed slaves. Neither of these sounded like jazz, and entrepreneurs resigned themselves to importing American talent, whatever the cost.

In 1925, at previews of yet another such show, *Revue nègre,* the management, dissatisfied with the dumpy, middle-aged blues singer sent to headline it, plucked young mixed-race dancer Josephine Baker from the chorus and re-fashioned her as its star. On 1 October, they previewed the show to backers and critics in a hastily created *danse sauvage*. Baker came on stage slung over the shoulder of Black dancer Joe Alex, he wearing only a posing pouch, she a few feathers. The effect was electric, repeated the following night's premiere at the 1900-seat Théâtre de Champs-Élysées. 'A scream of salutation spread through the theatre,' wrote Janet Flanner for *The New Yorker*. 'Her magnificent dark body proved to the French for the first time that Black was beautiful.' Joe Alex also had admirers. One magazine cartoon showed a sleeping middle-aged bourgeois couple, the man dreaming of Baker, his wife of Alex – who, ironically, was born in Belgium, and had never visited the United States.

Besieged by Parisian producers, Baker broke her contract and let the show travel on to Germany without her, signing instead with the Folies Bergère. As Paul Poiret, France's most chic designer, created a skirt of phallic velvet bananas for her début, cosmetician Helena Rubinstein, intuiting that, while Black might be beautiful, half-Black was even better, discreetly used body make-up to lighten her skin and make it appear more creamy.

Baker was an inadequate, if spirited, dancer and uninspired singer but her sexuality made up for these deficiencies. Once she recorded the tune that became her signature, *'J'ai Deux Amours'* (I Have Two Loves (My Country and Paris)), the French public not only accepted African-Americans but embraced them. The band leader of *Revue nègre*, clarinet and soprano saxophone virtuoso Sidney Bechet, moved to France, nucleus of a growing community of Black musicians. Eugene Bullard, former air ace and member of the French Foreign Legion, opened a Montmartre nightclub, as did mixed-race singer and dancer Ada Smith, known, because of her red hair, as Bricktop. Her patrons included Scott Fitzgerald, Cole Porter and the future King Edward VIII. While working in her kitchen, as yet unrecognized, was poet Langston Hughes, later a leading light of the Harlem Renaissance.

Off duty, African-American musicians and writers congregated at Café Tournon, in the shadow of that bastion of privilege, the Senate. The café became a magnet for women anxious to explore the possibilities of interracial sex. Black Americans who, back home, might be lynched for admiring a white ankle, could select partners from numerous attractive candidates. 'It was like having our own harem,' sighed novelist Chester Himes nostalgically.

After the Second World War, Paris became the jazz capital of Europe. American musicians who, because of criminal convictions, had lost the Cabaret Identification Card, which permitted them to perform in public, gravitated there. Among those who relocated were Chet Baker, Charlie 'Bird' Parker, Thelonious Monk, Billie Holiday and Bud Powell. A young jazz fan, Francis Paudras, befriended the schizophrenic and alcoholic Powell, and helped him perform and record again, a story Bertrand Tavernier told in his 1986 film *Round Midnight*, but with tenor saxophonist Dexter Gordon in the Powell role.

Centred on the Hôtel La Louisiane on rue de Seine, the Saint-Germain jazz scene brought together musicians, intellectuals and dilettantes in often unexpected combinations. Rothschild heiress Baroness Pannonica de Koenigswarter took Thelonious Monk and Charlie Parker under her wing. Parker met Jean-Paul Sartre at the Café Deux Magots and, after their conversation, told him, 'I'm very glad to have met you. I like your playing very much.' Sartre and Simone de Beauvoir patronized the Bal Nègre, a club in Montparnasse where working-class African emigrants gathered to dance with their white companions. Beauvoir laughed at the attempts of French intellectuals to mirror their lack of inhibition. 'Compared to the supple Africans and quivering West Indians,' she wrote, 'the stiffness of those who did was embarrassing. They looked like hysterics in a trance.'

Novelist Boris Vian, also a jazz trumpeter, acted as agent for such visiting musicians as the twenty-two-year-old Miles Davis, who arrived in Paris in 1949 and immediately fell in love with a beautiful young drifter named Juliette Gréco. 'I saw him in profile,' she recalled of her first glimpse. 'An Egyptian god. I had never seen such a handsome man. Like a Giacometti.' Their attraction was instant and profound. 'Music had been my whole life until Juliette,' Davis said. 'She taught me what it was like to love someone other than music.' They had only a few dozen words in common but that sufficed. He moved into Juliette's room at the Louisiane, launching a tradition that made the hotel a home-from-home for visiting jazz musicians. Her room was rare in having a bath, and Gréco remembered Davis sitting in it, playing music by the artist he called his 'darling' – Johann Sebastian Bach.

Gréco became the poster girl for left bank chic. One journalist noted that her 'clothes, fringe and unconventional behaviour (which includes walking the boulevards in bare feet and sitting on the kerb to rest) are faithfully copied by girls all over the quarter'. With her friend and sometime lover Anne-Marie Cazalis, she opened her own jazz club, the Tabou. From 1947, it occupied a cellar on narrow rue Dauphine, in the heart of the left bank. After a night of hectic jive to the band led by Vian, the unventilated crypt, thick with sweat and cigarette smoke, resembled a railway tunnel through which a steam locomotive had recently passed. Locals, furious at the noise of departing clients, emptied chamber pots onto their heads.

Sometimes, as the band took a break, the microphone passed to Gréco. 'She sang poems by Sartre and Jacques Prévert,' said a critic, 'in an odd deep voice, infinitely stirring to those under twenty-five and touchingly immature to those over thirty.' The songs were tailored to her rueful sexuality. Among the most successful was '*Déshabillez-moi*' (Undress Me).

As improved health, safety and noise abatement standards forced the closing of its more congested clubs, Paris dwindled as a jazz town. Miles Davis, irritated by the uncritical adulation of undiscriminating fans, returned to America. 'In Europe,' he complained, 'they like everything you do; the mistakes and everything. That's a little bit too much.' Django Reinhardt retired in 1951 and died shortly after, aged only forty-three, though his partner in the Quintette du Hot Club de France, violinist Stéphane Grappelli, performed for another thirty years. Ironically, *manouche* – Roma music, of the sort played by Reinhardt and Grappelli – would prove to be the French jazz that composers had sought three decades earlier. They'd been looking in the wrong place. While they searched for *le jazz hot*, Reinhardt and his compatriots invented *le jazz cool*.

In the vacuum left by the American diaspora, Paris became synonymous with the cerebral chamber jazz typified by the à cappella harmony of Ward Swingle's Double Six de Paris, later the Swingle Singers, Jacques Loussier's jazz transcriptions of Bach, and the big band compositions of Michel Legrand, who scored the jazz musicals *Les parapluies de Cherbourg* and *Les demoiselles de Rochefort*. In music of so little fire and much ice, the jungle beat of Josephine Baker seemed far away.

In 2022, Baker became the first American and the first show-business personality to be interred in the Panthéon. (Her body remains in Monaco, where she spent her last years as a guest of Princess Grace, the former Grace Kelly. Instead, the coffin contained earth from the three places of most significance in her life: Monaco, her birthplace of St Louis and Paris.) Her tomb can be visited in the crypt of the Panthéon. A square in Montparnasse is also named after her – and, incongruously, a *piscine* in the 13th arrondissement, though it's not known if she could even swim. The Latin Quarter has no monuments to Sartre and Beauvoir, but high on the wall at 33 rue Dauphine a tiny plaque identifies the former site of the Tabou.

A HORSEMAN ON A TOMATO

SURREALISM

In 1932, André Breton, founder and ideologue of the Surrealists – a name coined by Guillaume Apollinaire – set out to analyze the sexual habits of his followers. Both he and fellow member Paul Éluard had recently experienced bad break-ups, and Breton at least wondered why.

Breton began his enquiry after having been dumped by Suzanne Muzard, inspiration for the main character of his one 1928 novel, *Nadja*. Why she did so was implied in the first session, when novelist and poet Raymond Queneau asked, 'Do you always make love in the same way? If not, are the variations in order to increase your own pleasure or that of the woman?' Benjamin Péret, Jacques Prévert and Pierre Unik all agreed that the woman's pleasure was paramount. 'Like Péret,' Unik said, 'I always ask the woman what she prefers.' But Breton was astonished. 'I find that absolutely extraordinary, quite phenomenal. Talk about complications!'

'Surreal' is synonymous today with 'unreal' or 'improbable' but to the Surrealists it represented a state somewhere between the world we perceive and that of the imagination, a kind of waking dream in which we behave without rational thought. The movement grew out of the First World War. Breton, working in a hospital for victims of 'shell shock' (Post-traumatic Stress Disorder) noticed how some patients, despite having little education, conceived elaborate fantasies to rationalize their experiences. One believed that trench warfare was a pageant, with fake explosions and bodies supplied by mortuaries. Where did he get such ideas? Breton intuited that our unconscious was a reservoir of creativity, tapped only at times of unbearable stress, or while dreaming or in a hypnotic trance.

The son of a policeman, Breton was an unlikely leader for what became a radical and often violent movement. He disapproved of brothels and drugs, and was more interested in collecting and cataloguing art than exploring the unconscious. But having decided to do so, he went about it systematically. The group opened a Bureau of Surrealist Enquiries and invited people to visit and describe their dreams. Each afternoon, a discussion or séance took place in a Montmartre café. Attendance was obligatory. The only excuse for absence was that you were making love; sex was a force that even Breton recognized could not be denied.

Their hero was Isidore Ducasse, an obscure Franco-Uruguayan poet who called himself Comte de Lautréamont and died aged twenty-four in 1870. His imagery hinted at the possibility of expressing in words the apparent reality – or, rather, surreality – of the dream state. In an attempt to equal Ducasse's definition of 'convulsive love' as 'beautiful as the chance encounter of a sewing machine and an umbrella on an operating table', Breton volunteered 'the man who cannot visualize a horse galloping on a tomato is an idiot'.

Surrealism developed out of Dada, the playful philosophy conceived by Tristan Tzara while exiled to Switzerland during the war. Breton, in an effort to distance himself from Dada's jokes and games, embraced violence as a necessary adjunct to cultural revolution. 'The simplest act of surrealism,' he decreed, 'is to walk out into the street, gun in hand, and shoot at random.' No Surrealist went that far, but, to show its detestation of organized religion, some members, in particular Benjamin Péret, physically attacked priests and nuns in the street. If someone appeared to trespass on their territory, the group responded with violence. They disrupted the performance of German dancer Valeska Gert when she presented a programme of 'Surrealist Dance' and smashed the premises of a café calling itself Cabaret Lautréamont, even beating up the proprietor. (Breton apologized the next day, sending a letter on headed notepaper, to which he added a spot of blood, to show that he hadn't emerged from the event unscathed.)

The group scorned anything that set out to be Art with a capital 'A'. They rejected the experimental films of the time but praised pornography, slapstick and the gangster serials of Louis Feuillade. A favourite diversion, *cadavres exquis* (exquisite corpses), expanded the childhood game where one person drew a head, folded the paper and had someone else add a body, and a third the legs. They played it with sentences, naming it from one of their first successes '*Le cadavre exquis boira le vin nouveau*' (The exquisite corpse shall drink the new wine).

The group welcomed any opportunity *pour épater les bourgeois* (to impress the bourgeois), and Christmas 1929 presented them with just such a chance. The week before Christmas, in any French community, one knows to expect a visit from the postman, garbage collector, policeman and fireman. Ostensibly they are wishing you the compliments of the season and, as an expression of Christmas cheer, they offer an almanac. Card-covered, usually with an image of kittens or puppies, these contain some pious or inspirational texts, a calendar with the name of the saint for each day, plus the dates of Easter and other moveable feasts. You choose between the kittens and the dogs, offer a sum out of all proportion to the value of the item and close the door, free thereafter to ask a favour, and with no need to avoid their eye if you meet them in the street.

It was rare for any almanac to excite much comment, a fact that caught the attention of Breton and the Paris group in 1929. Gathered for their nightly séance, members were unsurprised to hear that the Brussels chapter of the Dadaists, their fellow travellers, was once again broke. For all his charm, its leader, gallerist Édouard Mesens, was hopeless in business.

The year before, they had rescued the group by compiling a special issue of its magazine *Variétés* with contributions from Breton, poet Louis Aragon and others, illustrated by Man Ray and René Magritte. It was Aragon's idea to do something similar by producing a salacious version of the humdrum almanac.

Aragon, Péret and even Breton wrote some smutty verses to set the tone. One began 'Ah the little girls who lift their skirts/ and diddle themselves in the bushes/ or in museums/ behind the plaster Apollos/ while their mother compares the statue's rod/ to her husband's/ and sighs ...'

Aragon showed these to Man Ray, and asked if he had anything to use as illustrations. Ray's relationship with Alice Prin, aka Kiki of Montparnasse, had recently ended when Henri Broca, publisher of the magazine *Paris-Montparnasse*, persuaded her she was sufficiently famous to write her memoirs, which he would publish. She and Broca became lovers. Succumbing to her own hype, Kiki dreamed of a movie career.

Ray showed Aragon some photographs of a couple having sex. Even with faces cropped out, it was obvious he and Kiki had posed for them, Ray tripping the shutter with a cable release. Aragon intuited why Ray was offering these images. If Kiki wanted fame, he'd give it to her, with a vengeance. To hate her so much, he mused, he must really love her.

The completed almanac, called simply *1929*, contained four groups of verse, named for the seasons, with a Ray photograph prefacing each. Mesens printed 215 copies in Brussels and shipped almost all of them to Paris, only to have the French *douane* seize the entire shipment at the border. Even so, copies were soon on sale clandestinely in both Paris and Brussels at inflated prices.

Inspired by one war, Surrealism expired with another. It began as a movement of writers but as Breton's autocratic manner alienated many supporters, he admitted artists and filmmakers such as Luis Buñuel and in particular Salvador Dalí, who was soon announcing, 'I *am* surrealism,' and touting himself to high-paying portrait clients and to Hollywood. Resentfully, Breton rearranged the letters of his name to spell 'Avida Dollars'. Breton, Dalí and others of the group took refuge in the Americas during the Nazi Occupation and, by the time they returned, Abstract Expressionism had overtaken Surrealism as the new vogue in art. Breton faded into the background. As he lamented to Luis Buñuel, 'You just can't shock people anymore.'

DEATH AND RESURRECTION

I In his poem 'Musée des Beaux Arts', W.H. Auden reminds us that disaster seldom comes when we expect it, but rather 'while someone else is eating or opening a window or just walking dully along'.

Nobody in Paris on 14 April 2019 expected the cathedral of Notre-Dame to burn; for fire to swirl around its two towers, and the sky to fill with a vast and spreading anvil of smoke. Undermined by flames, the *flèche* or 'arrow' in the middle of the roof, wrapped in steel scaffolding as part of a renovation, toppled ponderously into the nave. As workers dashed inside to rescue the treasures of eight centuries, the lead, now molten, that once kept water from the wooden rafters, dribbled and splashed around them, swift and silver as mercury, and hot enough to sear flesh. On the two towers, the gargoyles kept their backs to the flames, unwilling to believe the destruction taking place behind them. Fumes of burning ancient wood, plaster and gold leaf drifted over Paris: the stench of conflagration. People could only watch and weep.

Notre-Dame was no stranger to disaster. The tourists who queued every day to climb 387 steps to its south tower seldom spared a glance for the twenty-eight headless figures above the massive front doors, effigies of biblical elders who had maintained their vigil since the thirteenth century. Their heads were lopped off in the Revolution of 1789 by simple people who assumed that men and women with such expressions of lofty superiority must be kings and queens. (The heads were re-discovered in 1977, buried in the 9th arrondissement, and are now on display in the Musée de Cluny.)

One figure had nothing above his neck to start with. He cradled his severed head in his hands, its lips smiling serenely, while curling vines filled the space above his shoulders. Denis, patron saint of France, was decapitated by Romans who resented his followers destroying the temples of their gods. Legend has it that he rose to his feet after his execution, scooped up his head, and began to climb the hills north of the city. As he did so, his head delivered a sermon on the virtues of forgiveness. Later generations built a temple at the summit and called it the Montmartre (Mountain of the Martyr).

When, in 1830, twenty-nine-year-old Victor Hugo began to prowl here at night, demolition stalked the building with him. Even before

construction ended, about the time Columbus sailed for America, the oldest parts of the cathedral were crumbling. Rain from above and ground water from below eroded the mortar that gripped its stones, while in the intricate structure of oak beams that supported the roof, known as *la forêt* (the forest), the slow process of corruption was already advanced.

Muffled in a heavy coat that brushed the ground, Hugo roamed the dank crypts and staircases worn hollow by centuries of footsteps. Stonemasons got used to him standing in the shadows, making notes. They told him stories of characters from the past whose spirits still haunted the building, and his imagination did the rest.

One legendary foreman named Trajan suffered from kyphosis, a bone disease that cruelly twisted his spine. His workers had called him – though never in his hearing – M'sieur Bossu (Mr Hunchback). At dawn, as the doors opened for the first Mass of the day, Hugo hurried back to his little house, uncorked the giant bottle of ink he hoped would see him through the book and, within sight of the towers, began to write of Quasimodo, the deaf and twisted bell-ringer, and his passion for the Roma girl, Esmeralda, who danced where the tourists now queued, exciting the lust and fury of the priests within.

The novel he called *Notre-Dame de Paris*, but which gained international fame as *The Hunchback of Notre-Dame* – and, many believe, saved the cathedral from crumbling by alerting the public and the Church to its run-down state – was anything but subtle. It gave readers sex, violence and intrigue in surroundings drenched in both glamour and squalor. Hugo's medieval Paris is as gaudy and sadistic as *Game of Thrones*. Mothers and children separated at birth are miraculously reunited; saintly priests reveal themselves as the most dire of scoundrels. There are accusations of cannibalism, and the heroine ends up hanged. Above all, we relate to the character of Quasimodo, 'ugly, despised, appalling, solitary', who swings down to snatch the doomed Esmeralda and, amid cries of 'Sanctuary! Sanctuary!', carries her off to his lair.

The real hero of *Notre-Dame de Paris* is the cathedral itself; to Hugo a metaphor for France. He lamented the botched repairs and poorly built additions to the structure; the loss of the original Gothic altar, 'splendidly encumbered with shrines and reliquaries; with angels' heads and clouds', and the replacement of the stained glass of its ancient windows with 'cold, white panes'.

In 1842, the city hired twenty-eight-year-old architectural *wunderkind* Eugène-Emmanuel Viollet-le-Duc to restore Notre-Dame.

Before he could begin work, however, Louis-Napoleon Bonaparte, nephew of the first Napoleon, usurped the throne in a *coup d'état* and Hugo, once his supporter, now an opponent, took his family into exile, refusing to return so long as the now-Emperor Napoleon III remained in power. He could only watch from a distance as Viollet-le-Duc imposed his vision on the cathedral. Hugo applauded the restoration of the stained glass but scorned his addition of a faux-Gothic *flèche*, and the installation on the roof of twelve giant statues of the apostles – to which Viollet-le-Duc, not given to excessive modesty, added a thirteenth of himself.

Notre-Dame escaped complete destruction in 2019 by the skin of its teeth. Had flames reached the two towers, a new cathedral would almost certainly have risen on the site. But the decision was made to repair the original. Its rooftop statues were, fortunately, being refurbished elsewhere, and *pompiers* (firefighters) saved the windows by keeping their hoses away from the fragile stained glass. Although the flaming *flèche* and the beams of the *forêt* broke through the tracery of the inner roof, they left some of the stone vaulting intact. Even before the smoke cleared, plans were being made to restore to life the building, which, to most of the world, represents the spirit of France. It was here that Mary, Queen of Scots married the Dauphin François; where Napoleon I snatched the crown of France from the hands of Pope Pius VII and placed it on his own head; where the Requiem Mass for Charles de Gaulle was held. Future generations would never have forgiven those who let it crumble into ash.

TOWARDS A WHITE PARIS

THE 1962 MALRAUX LAW

A mong the thoroughfares leading downhill from Montmartre are rue Blanche (White Street) and Place Blanche (White Square). Both earned their name in another era. As carts rumbled down from the mines that honeycomb the *butte* (mound), dust from their loads drifted onto the verges, leaving a white crust. What they mined was gypsum, also known as alabaster. Soft and easily carved, it was an ideal material for tomb sculptures, portrait busts and other objects that remained indoors. In addition, when baked, ground to a powder and mixed with water, it became the tough, fire-resistant building material plaster of Paris, a key ingredient of drywall or Sheetrock.

Gypsum had been mined in Montmartre since Roman times, but by 1860 it was no longer profitable. The mines closed, leaving a honeycomb of tunnels. Georges-Eugène Haussmann, busily transforming Paris, gave up on Montmartre. Mining had made many areas unsafe, and its meandering streets, following tracks laid down over centuries, were ill-suited to his stately rows of apartment buildings. Instead, the locals, adapting paths worn by miners to carry their loads down the hillside, built wide staircases lined with townhouses, a solution that became one of the district's most distinctive features.

Like every imperial capital, Paris built to impress, each dynasty leaving behind a proof in stone of its power. This was nowhere more true than in the Basilica of Sacré-Coeur, on the summit of Montmartre, a symbol of the church's triumph over anarchy during the Commune. Its builders used travertine limestone. Extremely hard and fine grained, it exudes a white substance called calcite on contact with rainwater, giving the building its distinctive ethereal appearance. The presence of old mines, some cavernous enough to house a church on their own, forced engineers to go down 30m to find bedrock. The building rests on eighty-three shafts, filled with rock and concrete. Even if all the earth beneath it were removed, Sacré-Coeur would remain standing, as on stilts.

Montparnasse, on the opposite edge of the city, is riddled with the tunnels from which Italian masons quarried limestone for the façades of Haussmann's rebuilt city. It was this pale golden stone, almost as much as lighting in the streets, that earned Paris the title La Ville-Lumière (the City

ART AND CULTURE   51

of Light). The same respect for stone moved De Gaulle's Minister of Cultural Affairs, André Malraux, to create Law 62-903 in August 1962. It protected any French city threatened with redevelopment. Specifically, it saved the ancient Marais, on whose crumbling buildings and run-down alleys developers had cast greedy eyes for a century or more.

As early as 1922, the great architect Charles-Édouard Jeanneret-Gris (aka Le Corbusier) presented his vision of a new Paris, made up of sixty-storey skyscrapers spaced across a vast park, with a few historical sites – Place Vendôme, the Palais Royale, the Louvre – sentimentally preserved. There was less opposition than one might expect. Medieval Paris was dilapidated and crumbling. Hastily built additions were tacked on to palaces where kings once plotted and courtiers danced. Ancient banquet halls had become warehouses and, on courtyards turned into garages, sculptures carved under the Sun King looked down mournfully on gutted Citroën 2CVs. The Marais, in particular, was an eyesore. Many thought its demolition would be no loss.

Jean Giraudoux disagreed. In 1943, he wrote *The Madwoman of Chaillot*, a play about developers intent on drilling for oil on the heights of Trocadero, overlooking the Eiffel Tower. Their only opposition are outcasts – a street singer, a ragpicker, a sewer man and a flower girl – led by the madwoman of the title, Countess Aurelia, who dresses as she lives, in the style of a century before. Against all odds, the protestors succeed, using the smell of oil to lure the schemers into a bottomless pit.

In 1961 Le Corbusier re-submitted his plan to Malraux. The two were friends. Le Corbusier dedicated his book, *Le Corbusier: Les Plans de Paris*, to Malraux. But, if he had hoped for a sympathetic reception, he was disappointed. 'In our civilization,' Malraux decreed, 'the future does not oppose the past. It resurrects it.' (He hadn't always been such a stickler for conservation. In 1923, he, his wife and a confederate were arrested in Phnom Penh while trying to ship to France a tonne of sculptures looted from Cambodian temples. Facing a three-year prison sentence, he sent his wife back to Paris, where she persuaded Louis Aragon, André Gide and André Breton to sign a petition demanding privileged status for 'those who contribute to increasing the intellectual heritage of our country'. Their convictions were reduced to suspended sentences and they were allowed to return to France.)

Malraux not only rejected Corbusier's plan but launched an ambitious scheme to preserve old Paris, and in particular to refurbish the

Marais. In the process, later additions were torn down and old frontages revealed. The law stipulated that such façades, once exposed, must be conserved. If a shop had been a butcher a century ago, its original shopfront would be retained, even if it now sold *haute couture*. Above all, he ordered restoration of the stonework blackened by pollution and neglect. The law required that every building in Paris be steam-cleaned at least once a decade. The transformation was breathtaking. Within a few years it was once again a city of light. When he handed his portfolio to his successor, Françoise Giroud, Malraux told her expansively, 'Behold! I bequeath you a white Paris.' It's white still.

A TOWER TOO FAR

EIFFEL AND HIS MONUMENT

In February 1912, an Austrian tailor named Franz Reichelt stood uncertainly on the first level of the Eiffel Tower. The frozen ground 60m below looked hard, but he told himself repeatedly that the folds of the silk suit he'd sewn so meticulously would slow his fall and win the prize offered by the Aéro-Club de France for the first practical parachute. Friends urged him to use a dummy, but Reichelt insisted on jumping himself, to show there was no trickery. It took long moments of hesitation and false starts before he launched himself – but only a few seconds to reach the ground. The Eiffel Tower had claimed another victim.

Paris's signifying emblem and the world's most popular paid tourist attraction, the tower is as instantly identifiable as the Apple computer symbol or the Coca-Cola wave. Kings and presidents have dined in it, social and architectural critics attacked it, thrill-seekers and suicides kept their rendezvous with oblivion within its cast-iron embrace. Seven million visitors a year ascend to its first level. A smaller and more energetic group reach the summit – 300m above the ground – to find, to their surprise, a reproduction of Eiffel's office, with wax models of Eiffel and his daughter Claire welcoming fellow inventor Thomas Alva Edison, who admired Eiffel and visited him in Paris. Despite what the authorities call 'the most draconian safety standards', there continue to be suicides. A spokesperson will say only that 'there are

years where there may have been two or three, but also years where there is nothing at all'.

From the start, there was something both ridiculous and terrible about this harbinger of twentieth-century technology. When, in 1886, the city of Paris invited ideas for a monument to celebrate the centenary of the 1789 Revolution, Gustave Eiffel, France's greatest engineer, initially turned down the plan proposed by associates for a tower taller than any yet built, and made entirely from iron. He was finally persuaded, but his doubts persisted, mirrored by others.

As soon as work began on the Champ de Mars, the former military parade ground beside the Seine, influential figures expressed their disapproval. One suggested that any true monument to the Revolution should take the form of a giant guillotine, to recognize the role of that device in the slaughter of La Terreur. A Committee of Three Hundred (one member for each metre of the tower's height) rallied celebrities opposed to Eiffel's design, among them Charles Garnier, architect of the Paris Opéra, composers Charles Gounod and Jules Massenet, author Guy de Maupassant and painter William-Adolphe Bouguereau. 'Imagine for a moment,' suggested their petition, 'a giddy, ridiculous tower dominating Paris like a gigantic black smokestack, crushing under its barbaric bulk Notre-Dame, the Tour Saint-Jacques, the Louvre, the dome of Les Invalides, the Arc de Triomphe. All of our humiliated monuments will disappear in this ghastly dream.' Maupassant remained opposed even after it was built – though he did, he said dryly, enjoy eating in its restaurant: one of the few places where the tower couldn't be seen.

It wasn't until the First World War that people got used to the tower, which by then had become part of the life of Paris, known familiarly as *La dame de fer* (the Iron Lady). With the Germans dug in only 65km away, close enough for their aircraft to make bombing raids and their mighty Paris-Geschuts (Paris Gun) to bombard it, the army used the summit as a listening post. Among the messages it intercepted were those to the high command in Berlin that exposed dancer and courtesan Mata Hari as a spy.

After the war, radio stations broadcast from its summit and aircraft navigated on its signals. One even flew through its base arch. Between 1929 and 1935, automobile manufacturer Citroën paid to have its name spelled out in lights by night. People were married on it, inspiring Jean Cocteau's 1921 ballet *Les Mariés de la Tour Eiffel*. In 1923, journalist Pierre Labric, as publicity for his newspaper, rode a bicycle down the 347 steps from the first level. In 1924, filmmaker René Clair used it as the setting for his fantasy *Paris Qui Dort* (Paris Which Sleeps). A scientist invents a ray that puts everyone in Paris to sleep except passengers in an aircraft and the watchman on the Eiffel Tower, where the group take refuge, bickering, flirting and making occasional excursions into the sleeping city.

Eiffel joined the tower's beams with bolts rather than welding them, since everyone assumed it would be demolished after the 1889 Exposition Universelle. In 1925, a swindler named Victor Lustig spotted an opportunity. Claiming to represent the Ministère de Postes et Télégraphes, he informed France's leading scrap metal merchants that 'because of engineering faults, costly repairs, and political problems I cannot discuss, the tearing down of the Eiffel Tower has become mandatory'. Bids were invited for the contract. Lustig then hinted to the greedier that he might be open to a bribe. One dealer paid him a large sum for preferential treatment, after which Lustig, convinced the swindled man would report him to the police, fled the country. When the mark proved too embarrassed to report the scam to the police and thus reveal his humiliation, Lustig returned and tried to work the swindle again, again escaping one step ahead of the law.

In 1940, as a last futile gesture before German forces entered Paris, tower staff cut the cables of its elevator. Hitler planned to survey the captured city from the summit but, faced with the climb, changed his mind. The cables weren't repaired until 1946. Throughout the Occupation, sentries stood guard at ground level. With nobody ready to climb 1,710 steps to the summit, the Resistance was free to broadcast clandestine messages from its radio antenna.

Today, the tower is more popular than ever. Armoured glass has replaced the floor of the first level, so tourists looking down between their feet can share the last sight of Franz Reichelt and the other 400 people who have leaped from there to their deaths. In 2000, the city installed 20,000 halogen bulbs that continue, every hour on the hour, to cloak it in shimmering light. Some still regret they didn't also accept the suggestion of a wit that, since the bottom-heavy form of the tower made it appear to be squatting, it should mark the millennium by laying a giant egg. Guy de Maupassant would have been the first to applaud.

The tower continued to tempt daredevils and those afflicted with a death wish. Applications to climb it are routinely denied. Only GREP, the deep exploration and research group, a specialized unit of the Paris firefighters, is allowed, once a month, to use it to practise abseiling.

Parachutists and sky divers periodically evade the guardians, undeterred by the fact that 800m is regarded as the lowest safe height from which to attempt a base jump. In 2003, veteran Hervé le Gallou successfully parachuted from the summit. In 2005, police arrested two Norwegians as they attempted the same feat to advertise a line of clothing. Another hid and tried again that night – fatally, since the wind carried him into collision with the lower structure and he died instantly. In 2023, a twenty-four-year-old Frenchman became the latest person to achieve what Franz Reichelt died attempting in 1912. He's unlikely to be the last.

MY PARISIAN PAVEMENT
BELGIAN BLOCKS AND HAUSSMANN COBBLES

Among the strangest souvenirs one can take back home from a visit to Paris is a cube of grey granite, of the kind that covers most of its streets. Each is machine cut and weighs more than 1kg. They come hand-painted with '*Mon Pavé Parisien*' (My Parisian pavement) but also coated in gold: definitely a gift for The Person Who Has Everything.

What's so special about a cobblestone? A great deal, in fact, since without them, modern Paris would not exist.

Few of us today would recognize Paris around 1850. The wealthy, most of whom lived off revenue from their country estates, seldom left their *hôtels particuliers* (private mansions) except to visit other families who enjoyed the same comfortable seclusion. To do so, they travelled by coach or on horseback, ignoring what took place on the streets.

Shopping was done by servants. These poorly paid men and women set out each day, returning with the ingredients to feed their employers. It was not a Paris that took notice of passing trade, since there wasn't any. Few shops had frontages, but were simply open storerooms or cellars, hung with carcasses or piled with vegetables. Oil, beer and wine came by the barrel, flour by the sack. Some merchants set up tables in the street to sell produce grown in the farms surrounding Paris, which carts carried in each night for distribution at the huge central market known as Les Halles.

Only about a fifth of its streets were paved. The rest were mud in winter and dust in summer, both liberally mixed with excrement – animal and human. At busier street corners, some husky locals loitered, ready, for a few sous, to piggy-back one across the worst of it. The few paved streets were surfaced with so-called Belgian blocks. Each about the size of a human head, they were chiselled by hand and cemented together, but often gave way under a loaded cart or coach. When Napoleon III made Georges-Eugène Haussmann *préfet* of the Île de Paris region, his first job, after building a sewer system and otherwise modernizing the city, was to widen and pave its streets. To do so, he introduced smaller granite cubes, identically machine cut, but with two improvements. Instead of cementing them together, he left them loose and, rather than seating them on gravel, bedded them in sand. The weight of a cart would never rest on more than a few at a time, and the sand would absorb the pressure.

Almost no one appreciated Haussmann's ingenuity until Parisians revolting against German Occupation in 1944 found they could tear up the blocks to create barricades. In 1968, dissident students, seeking projectiles to throw at the police and militia, made the same discovery. As *les evenements de '68* were as much about theatre as politics, their delight at having such readily available missiles was soon visible on the city's walls as the graffito *'Sous les pavés, la plage!'* (Under the cobbles, a beach!).

Not everyone welcomed Haussmann's innovations. British novelist Ford Madox Ford attacked the perceived emptiness and lack of character in 'Haussmannised' streets. The grating of metal wheels on the new cobbles irritated some residents of elegant riverside addresses, who first strewed them with straw, then demanded their replacement with blocks of wood. This backfired in 1910, when the Seine flooded. The wood blocks swelled and their streets became impassable.

Clearing space for new buildings, workmen had to demolish deconsecrated churches, excavate cemeteries and dig out plague pits dating back to the Black Death. They piled the bones into carts and hauled them to Montparnasse, where Louis-Étienne Héricart de Thury, Director of the Paris Mine Inspection Service (and evidently something of a ghoul) had transformed abandoned underground quarries into an ossuary (a burial site), lining the tunnels with orderly arrangements of skulls and femurs. He also created a museum showing skeletons that exhibited genetic or disease-generated deformities. Over the door to the labyrinth, a stone tablet warned sternly *'Arrête! C'est ici l'empire de la Mort'* (Stop! This is the empire of death).

Tunnels still honeycomb large areas of Montparnasse, revealing their presence only when a sink-hole opens and part of a street disappears.

The section designated as the Catacombs, at Place Denfert-Rochereau, and open to tourists, represents only a small part of the 280km network. Alert visitors will notice bolted gates leading to passages wandering further into the dark. Accessible only through manholes scattered across the district are caverns decorated with wall art that suggests their use in some occult ritual. Members of the Resistance also met here. One gallery contained an abandoned cinema with electric lighting, seats and projectors. Secret *cinéastes* (those knowledgeable about the cinema)? Or a briefing room where criminals and terrorists watched films of their next target? The empire of death has yet to divulge all its secrets.

FOOD AND DRINK

SNAILS

On the road across Picardy, heading for Calais and the cross-Channel ferry to Britain, one will pass, on any warm, moist day, scores of people along the roadside, plastic bags in hand. They are gathering snails, which they'll bake with garlic, parsley and butter in one of French cuisine's traditional specialities. But on the British side, while the landscape, weather and, presumably, the snails are identical, the verges are deserted. The British, who eat eels, tripe, pigs' feet and haggis, draw the line at snails.

Admittedly it's a challenge to prepare the fat, brown Burgundy gastropod, *Helix pomatia*, for the table. They first have to be starved, to cleanse their digestive tract. Some set them loose on trays of flour, but American food writer M.F.K. Fisher watched a different method in Dijon. Scores of snails were placed on a sheet of glass which was then suspended upside down over a box. 'For a day or two, they stayed,' she recalled, 'bottoms up, on the glass. Then they began to drop off. Nights were punctuated with the thumps of snails fainting in their little black hole. We lost sleep, feeling very sick for them, waiting for the hunger swoon to overcome another and another.' Having expired, their meat could be extracted, trimmed, replaced in the shells, and baked. Was it worth the effort? This misses the point. *Escargots à la Bourguignonne* conform almost exactly to a French need to find food in everything nature can afford. The dish is as much symbol as sustenance.

Snails also made an unexpected appearance in the annals of science. There were years during the nineteenth century when every month seemed to bring a new discovery, each, superficially, as credible as the last. If moving pictures or the telephone could exist, why not levitation? Or fairies? So when Jacques Toussaint Benoît suggested in 1850 that snails possessed a telepathic bond which could be adapted into a form of communication, he wasn't immediately mocked.

Benoît claimed that snails mated for life, and that each couple shared a 'sympathetic fluid', so that, if you did something to one, its partner, however distant, would react with what he called an 'escargotic commotion'. It followed that, if you placed a letter next to one snail and gave it an electric shock, its partner would respond. Messages could then be spelled out and sent by, literally, 'snail mail'.

Working with an American named Biat-Chrétien, Benoît built a prototype of his pasilalinic-sympathetic compass or snail telegraph, and held a demonstration for potential investors. Twenty-four pairs of mated escargots, each representing a letter, were placed in zinc bowls nailed to 10-ft wooden beams, and the beams separated by a curtain. In theory, if a snail representing letter 'A' was jabbed with electricity on one side of the curtain, its opposite number would react. Using this system, Benoît was able to transmit the words '*gymnase*' as '*gymoate*' and '*lumiere divine*' as '*lumhere divine*' – results promising enough to raise financing for further development. Investors, however, noticed that Benoît and Biat-Chrétien slipped back and forth through the curtain during the experiment. Before they put up more money, they demanded another test under controlled conditions and more stringent oversight. Such an experiment was announced, but Benoît failed to show. He died two years later in Paris, penniless, and his pasilalinic-sympathetic compass was never heard of again.

DON'T EAT THE FEET

THE ORTOLAN

The French spend more time eating and drinking than any other country in the world; in excess of two hours a day, against the UK's 1 hour 18 minutes, Australia's 1 hour 31 minutes, and the United States' 1 hour and 1 minute. This doesn't mean they eat more; they just take more time doing it. The mechanics of eating mean far more than what they actually consume. As Henry Higgins says in *My Fair Lady*, 'The French don't care what they do actually, as long as they *pronounce* it correctly'.

The American ideal of eating – pizza, hamburgers, ribs, steak – is predicated on quantity and ease of consumption, whereas the French take pleasure a number of short courses, eaten slowly. Few cuisines are as labour-intensive. The time and expertise required to prepare and eat a snail is out of all proportion to what goes into one's mouth. A soufflé is an omelette that takes an hour to prepare. Proud as the French are of their almost thousand cheeses, they eat them only a sliver at a time.

Haute cuisine can sometimes seem to be concerned more with the intricacy of preparation and the aesthetics of presentation of the dish than its taste. For a 1908 dinner in Paris at which the Prince of Wales was guest of honour, *chef de cuisine* Georges Auguste Escoffier created Nymphs à l'Aurore (Nymphs in the Dawn), a dish that paid tribute to the Prince's sensual and erotic character. In clear champagne jelly, tiny morsels of meat, tinted pale pink – actually frogs' legs coated in a creamy sauce – peeped from green fronds in a tantalizing suggestion of female creatures wreathed in water plants. This dish is often described but nobody mentions its taste. Perhaps they didn't actually eat it, but just sat and admired it.

Whatever they consume, however, they prefer, overwhelmingly, that it be French. 'The French do not love any food which is not their own – meaning not of their region, let alone not of their country,' observed writer Celia Brayfield. 'Persuading a provincial French family to swap green beans for Brussels sprouts is almost impossible.' Other countries, indifferent to source, prefer a standard item, available all year round, while the French, alert to season and region, prefer the first French Gariguette strawberries to Spanish imports, and await the appearance of local asparagus or green beans, even when equivalents from Israel or Kenya are available, often at a lower price.

Despite this, the width and breadth of the national appetite remains impressive. The French sometimes seem to take a perverse pleasure in eating things others discard. Oscar Wilde's jibe that 'The English country gentleman galloping after a fox' was a case of 'the unspeakable in full pursuit of the uneatable' might apply to the French cook in search of the edible. As with the fox hunt, however, the merit is in the chase. Not everyone can be bothered digging out the tender 'oysters' of flesh found near the backbone of a chicken or turkey, but packs of these nuggets are sold in supermarkets with the somewhat smug label '*Le sot-l'y-laisse*' (The stupid leave them).

It's to this adventurousness in sourcing ingredients that we owe many foods now taken for granted. Scots traveller John Lauder, visiting France in 1665, was disgusted by the sight of people eating mushrooms. 'It astonished me that the French find them so delicious. They gather them at night in the most sordid and damp places. They cook them in a terrine with butter, vinegar, salt and spices. If you have them grilled, you can imagine you are biting into the tenderest meat. But I was so biased that I couldn't eat them.'

Nor would everyone immediately see a meal in *Emberiza hortulana*, a tiny bird of the bunting family, known as the ortolan. These creatures, each about the size of a thumb, were caught in mist nets, fattened up, then drowned in Armagnac before being roasted in twos or threes in individual ceramic containers. Each diner received a dish, which they opened only after draping a large napkin over their heads to conserve the aroma. Then they ate the birds whole, including downy feathers, intestines and beak – though it was considered a sign of elegance to leave the feet.

Trapping or eating ortolan is now a criminal offence, but the bird wasn't declared a protected species until 1999. This coincided with accounts of the farewell banquet hosted by a dying François Mitterrand, at which the former President, recalled writer Michael Paterniti, enjoyed 'the meal's ultimate course: a small, yellow-throated songbird that was illegal to eat. Rare and seductive, the bird – ortolan – supposedly represented the French soul. And this old man, this ravenous president, had taken it whole – wings, feet, liver, heart. Swallowed it, bones and all. Consumed it beneath a white cloth so that God Himself couldn't witness the barbaric act.'

In the context of French cuisine, the ortolan was not outrageously exotic. In 1871, when the army of Prussia laid siege to the city for five months, people found food where they could. After cows, chickens and sheep disappeared, it was the turn of the city's 25,000 cats, followed by dogs and rats. Restaurants served terrine of rat and donkey meat, roasted leg of dog, dogs' brains, and saddle of cat with mayonnaise. Horses were next. Despite relying on them for transport and haulage, Parisians would eventually consume an estimated 70,000. Even the emperor succumbed. Two thoroughbreds, a gift from Tsar Alexander II, provided meals for the imperial court.

When the Jardins d'Acclimatation, Paris's zoo, could no longer feed its animals and offered them for sale as livestock, butchers snapped up deer, antelopes and bear, all known to be edible. M. Deboos, at the Boucherie Anglaise on Boulevard Haussmann, also bought a yak. Under all that hair, it was, after all, a kind of buffalo, and could pass for beef. Lions and tigers found no buyers, nor did chimpanzees and other primates: the recent publication of Darwin's *On the Origin of Species* prejudiced even the French against consuming creatures to which they might, however distantly, be related. Nor were there any takers for a hippopotamus. Who knew if the blubbery beast was even edible? But M. Deboos paid 27,000 francs for two elephants, a treat for local gourmets. Their flesh made a good *bouillon* and the blood a passable *boudin noir* (black pudding) but they particularly relished the tender meat of the trunk. (Deboos may have read Jules Verne's

Five Weeks in a Balloon, published in 1863, in which aeronauts travelling across Africa descend to eat a meal of elephant trunk.)

The French recognize three categories of eater – the gourmet, the gourmand and the gastronome. Gastronomes eat almost nothing. Concerned primarily with assessing and maintaining standards of taste, they just nibble and move on. Gourmets come closest to the norm. They enjoy food, take pleasure in the act of eating, and may even, occasionally, over-indulge but don't in general concern themselves with food between meals.

Which leaves the gourmand – the glutton. Normally, one wouldn't expect to class the great Escoffier among this group. Spending the day in the kitchen, stirring, chopping, tasting, is the easiest way to ruin one's appetite.

Yet consider his description of the meals he consumed at a shooting party in the Haute-Savoie just before the First World War:

> Our dinner was composed of a cream of pumpkin soup with little croutons fried in butter, a young turkey roasted on the spit, accompanied by a large country sausage and a salad of potatoes, dandelions and beetroot, and followed by pears cooked in red wine and served with whipped cream. Dinner next day consisted of a cabbage, potato, and kohlrabi soup, augmented with three young chickens, an enormous piece of lean bacon, and a big farmhouse sausage. The broth, with some of the mashed vegetables, was poured over slices of toast, which made an excellent rustic soup. To follow, we were served with a leg of mutton, tender and pink, accompanied by a purée of chestnuts. An immense, hermetically sealed terrine gave out, when uncovered, a marvellous scent of truffles, partridges, and aromatic herbs. This terrine contained eight young partridges, amply truffled and wrapped in fat bacon, a little bouquet of mountain herbs and several glasses of fine champagne cognac. The next day's luncheon was composed partly of the trophies of the previous day's shooting [apparently 'three hares, a very young chamois, eleven partridges, three capercailzies, six young rabbits, and a quantity of small birds']. We did not have any *hors-d'oeuvre* but instead, some char [a freshwater fish, resembling a salmon], cooked and left to get cold in white wine from our host's own vineyards.

Nobody in France eats on this scale any longer. An echo survives, however, in *menus de degustation* or tasting menus. These cruises through the imagination of a *chef de cuisine* can be a trial of a quite different sort. One of Paris's most distinguished chefs invited a group of food writers to sample his expertise. As they were still chatting and catching up, the first of ten courses was served and, following a suitable pause, a second. At this point, they noticed they'd been given the first course all over again, and demanded an explanation. After consulting his boss, the waiter reported, severely, 'Chef says that, when you ate it the first time, you weren't paying attention.'

THE ART OF FRENCH PASTRY

T o call anything 'French' implies superiority in taste or style. French lace is the most delicate, French perfume the most complex, French pastry the perfection for which all *pâtissiers* strive. When it comes to the *éclair*, the *tarte aux pommes*, the *millefeuille*, how could the doughnut, the rock cake or the Twinkie compete? The country that produced Marie-Antoine Carême has no need to look over its shoulder. A second-place runner wasn't even in sight.

When Napoleon I decided to turn a chateau at Valençay on the Loire into a centre for diplomatic dining, he made it the responsibility of his Minister for Europe and Foreign Affairs, arch-intriguer Charles Maurice de Talleyrand-Périgord. Ordered to entertain at least four times a week, with never fewer than thirty-six guests, Talleyrand, inspired by the new emperor's transformation of the French state, set his chef, Carême, a challenge – to create a menu for every day of the year which, as well as respecting the religious restrictions of Lent and meat-less Fridays, used only ingredients then in season. Carême, delighted to show off his expertise, did so with ease.

After Napoleon abdicated and foreign troops occupied Paris, Talleyrand realized that if Tsar Alexander I were to occupy the vacant Élysée Palace, he would become, *de facto*, the head of state. So he circulated a rumour that the building was mined and invited Alexander to enjoy the hospitality of his home instead – and the cooking of Carême. The Tsar – whose troops were pounding the tables of Paris's cafés and, by demanding food '*Bwystra*' (Fast), adding *bistro* to the French vocabulary – was so delighted by what he ate that he took Carême back to Russia, where the chef, seeing the unlimited manpower available to an absolute monarch, introduced what became known as Russian service. Instead of every dish being brought to the table at the same time and diners helping themselves, each individual received a plate, served at the same moment by a regiment of waiters. It's the system still employed in France today.

Had he done nothing but invent *choux* pastry, the immortality of Carême would be assured. Made from flour, melted butter, eggs and water, and called *choux* (cabbage) because of its tendency to assume a globular form, it contains no baking powder or yeast. In the oven, water becomes steam, inflating the paste into an almost weightless shell, ready to accept *chantilly*, *crème pâtissière*, chocolate sauce, ice-cream, even cheese.

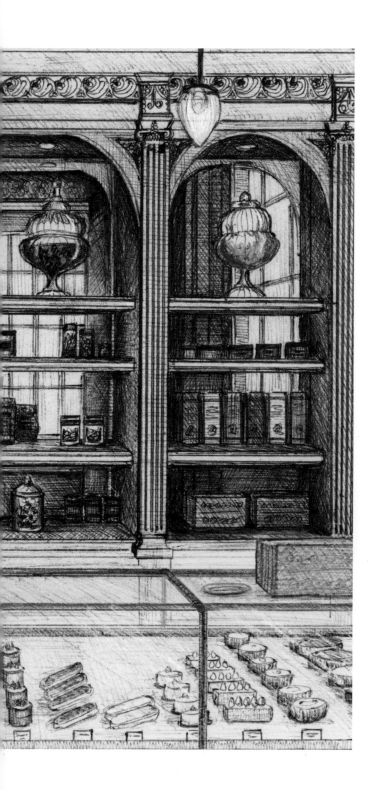

Choux is the basis of the *éclair*, the *profiterole*, the *gougère*. In 1910, to celebrate an epic bike race to Paris from Brest, France's furthest western city, a chef extended the length of an eclair and joined the ends in a ring, suggestive of a bicycle wheel, then split it horizontally, filled it with praline cream and scattered flaked almonds on top to create the Paris-Brest. Another *pâtissier* perched a small *choux* puff on a larger sphere, filled both with *crème pâtissière*, frosted them in caramel and, since the result resembled a nun in her habit, called them *religieuses*. Whereupon a competitor created a single sphere, also cream-filled, and christened it *pets de nonne* (a nun's fart).

Nothing takes the glamour out of eating pastry more quickly than using a knife or fork. *Choux*, in particular, doesn't cut cleanly. It compresses, leading to unseemly oozing. To employ one's fingers in eating cake is *de rigueur*. Partly it's down to the French aversion to crumbs; hence a liking for almond flour that keeps cakes dense and intact, without leaving a residue on one's clothing. At one time, to eat *pâtisserie* with fingers alone was a custom observed everywhere. For an episode of the TV series *Downton Abbey*, in which the youngest daughter of the aristocratic family decides to make a cake, the producer recalled, 'We shot the cake on the table with plates, forks and napkins' – at the sight of which the series' chief writer Julian Fellowes intervened. 'He's a historian as well as a writer,' the producer continued. 'He said the upper classes would eat with their fingers.' She sighed. 'Apparently it was true.' The cast tried, but it looked so wrong that, authentic or not, the scene was never shown.

THE RISE OF LE COCKTAIL

Today, the bars of Paris take mixed drinks for granted, but before Americans began ordering them in the 1920s, France knew nothing of cocktails. Anyone asking for a Martini and expecting gin with a dash of vermouth and an olive received instead something sweet and red, smelling of sage, garnished with a slice of orange – and absent, naturally, ice.

If French people met for a drink in what would become known as the 'cocktail hour', it was for an *aperitif*, a glass of wine with some infusion of herbs, meant to sharpen the appetite. Most people, however, associated *le cinq à sept* (the five to seven) not with drinking but sex. A man would leave his office at five, visit his mistress and enjoy her company for a few hours before heading home to his wife and children for family dinner.

Not only were cocktails unknown, but the French lacked the ingredients to make them. The use of wine as part of the Catholic Mass made the church in France a major consumer, so most abbeys devoted themselves to viticulture. It was left to foreign distillers to ferment grain and sugar cane to produce whisky, gin and rum. The only *eau de vie* readily available in France was brandy, and despite Samuel Johnson's assertion that 'claret is the *liquor* for boys, port for men, but he who aspires to be a *hero* must drink *brandy*', many drinkers, finding its nickname 'the Infuriator' well chosen, looked for ways to reduce or vary its effects.

In Charente, home of cognac, producers diluted it with fermented grape juice to make Pineau. Elsewhere, monks infused brandy or wine with flowers and herbs in 'fortified' cordials. These were sipped in small quantities before meals to stimulate appetite – *aperitifs* – or, after eating, to aid digestion – *digestifs*. Among the most famous were Benedictine, created by the monks of that order, and Chartreuse, developed in a monastery near Grenoble. A mixture of 130 herbs and flowers gave it a distinctive yellow-green tint that became recognized as a colour in its own right. Once cocktails took off, French-made *liqueurs* proliferated. In Scott Fitzgerald's *Tender is the Night*, Dick Diver contemplates a typical bar, furnished with 'the humbler poisons of France – bottles of Otard, Rhum St James, Marie Brizzard, Punch Orangeade, André Fernet Branca, Cherry Rochet, and Armagnac'.

When, in 1920, Prohibition halted the production and consumption of alcohol in the United States, its citizens turned thirstily towards more liberal

Europe. 'To a certain class of American,' wrote Jimmie Charters, barman at Paris's Jockey, Dingo and Harry's Bar, 'drinking in excess became an obligation. No party was a success without complete intoxication of the guests.' Journalist Waverley Root, arriving from New York to take up a job on the *Herald Tribune*, followed what he understood was a French custom and ordered a bottle of *vin rouge* with his first continental meal. The waiter didn't feel it was his business to explain that even the French didn't drink wine with breakfast.

So-called *bars américains* appeared all over Paris, offering highballs, toddies, fizzes, sours, juleps and coolers. In addition to the classic Martini, Cosmopolitan, Stinger and Manhattan, barmen might be asked to produce the Corpse Reviver (gin, Cointreau and absinthe), Satan's Whiskers (Italian and French vermouth, gin, orange juice and Grand Marnier), the Josephine Baker (cognac, apricot brandy, port, lemon zest and an egg yolk) and even one named for Napoleon, a blend of gin with dashes of the bitter *digestif* Fernet Branca, the *aperitif* Dubonnet, and citrus liqueur Curaçao. 'Our epoch,' announced Dutch painter Kees van Dongen in 1928, 'is the cocktail epoch. Cocktails! They are of all colours. They contain something of everything. The modern society woman is a cocktail. Society itself is a bright mixture. You can blend people of all tastes and classes.'

The proprietor of one bar on the Champs-Élysées, to help his staff with difficult customers, invented forty recipes for 'American drinks', each with a number. When a client asked for something of which the barman had never heard, he'd show him the list. If he still wasn't satisfied, an individual dressed in deep black, known as 'the Doctor', was summoned. Solemnly taking the client's pulse, he indicated the concoction he felt suited his needs.

Gin and whisky took some time to catch on in France. Both were preceded by rum, imported from Haiti and taken up in the form of toddy or punch. Combining rum, hot water, sugar and lemon, it was rumoured to offer protection from the insidious infection known as *la grippe*. 'And we sit outside the Dôme Café,' Ernest Hemingway wrote to Sherwood Anderson, 'warmed up against one of those charcoal braziers and it's so damned cold outside and the brazier makes it so warm and we drink rum punch, hot, and the rum enters into us like the Holy Spirit.'

The best rum was aged to evaporate excess alcohol and filtered to remove impurities. Less care was taken with tafia, the crude spirit, straight out of the still, which retained 60 per cent alcohol, along with a rich catalogue of poisons. (To test potency, one mixed some with gunpowder and applied a match. The good stuff exploded.) But being strong and cheap made it ideal for use by the French army during the First World War. Infantry men moving up to the line carried two metal canteens, each of a litre, one filled with a mixture of water and red wine, the other with tafia. In addition, when they were about to go 'over the top', officers sometimes doled out an additional tot, *pour rendre fou* (to make them crazy).

Another spirit earned an even more controversial reputation. Infusing alcohol with anise, fennel and the bitter herb *Artemisia absinthium* – the biblical wormwood – created absinthe. Pale green and translucent, with the taste of liquorice, it contained 70 per cent alcohol, against the 40 per cent of whisky and gin.

Sometimes poor distillation failed to extract every drop of thujone, an alkaloid that could adversely affect the brain. Addicts called absinthe *la fée verte* (the green fairy) for its capacity to cloud the mind and induce delusions. Habitual users dared less adventurous friends to try it. 'Why don't you take some absinthe?' demanded playwright August Strindberg. 'Are you afraid of it? Look at the bottle! It's marked with the Geneva [Red] cross! It heals those who have been wounded on the battlefield, friends and foes alike; it dulls all pain, blunts the keen edge of thought, blots out memories, stifles all the nobler emotions which beguile humanity into folly, and finally extinguishes the light of reason.' Strindberg spoke from experience. Shortly after his friend Paul Verlaine succumbed to its effects, he showed composer Frederick Delius a photograph of the poet on his deathbed and asked what he saw.

'Such as?'

'Well, the huge animal lying on his stomach,' Strindberg said, puzzled at the other's obtuseness, 'and the imp crouched on the floor!'

To modify its effect, one trickled water into the spirit through a sugar cube, halting when the mixture became cloudy. Serious drinkers skipped this step entirely, while those even more dangerously inclined could risk Ernest Hemingway's recipe for a cocktail he called Death in the Afternoon: 'Pour one jigger absinthe into a champagne glass. Add iced champagne until it attains the proper opalescent milkiness. Drink three to five of these slowly.'

Absinthe was so potent that the French government outlawed it in 1915, claiming it sapped the will of recruits to the army, making them disinclined to face German machine guns. Distillers ceased production. Stocks dwindled until the spirit became unobtainable. For half a century, absinthe existed in a limbo of fantasy and speculation until a few surviving bottles, unearthed from forgotten caves, allowed researchers to analyze the contents and recreate the formula. It's now readily available, and some Paris bars specialize in absinthe-related cocktails, served with appropriate ceremony, including Art Nouveau carafes of silver and glass with which to trickle ice water into the tantalizing green spirit.

With 'cocktail' now the accepted designation for any drinks event, from sipping a modest *pastis* with friends to a post-wedding debauch, the French interest in new and exotic libations has widened and deepened. When the 1960s brought increased immigration from the French Antilles, certain street markets in the Paris suburbs assumed a strong Caribbean character. Next to heaps of Jamaican meat patties and spicy salt-cod-batter *accras* were large glass vessels of murky yellow-green fluid in which floated objects of indeterminate character and origin. Ingredients included star anise, cinnamon, cloves, ginger, but mostly rum. This so-called punch, pronounced 'ponch', brewed at home and sold by the glass, wasn't meant to be drunk hot, as in Hemingway's time, but rather on a warm day, in a long glass, over ice. It soon became so popular that commercially bottled versions appeared.

Another phenomenon of drinking post-Second World War was the popularity of the *aperitif* kir (pronounced 'keer'). The recipe was simple. To a flute of white wine, Aligoté Burgundy for preference, add a shot of *crème de cassis*, a syrup made from blackcurrants. The drink was named for its inventor, Félix Kir, a canon of the Catholic church, leader of the wartime anti-Nazi Resistance around Dijon, where he was mayor from 1945 until his death in 1968. A pioneer in 'twinning' towns, Dijon was linked to Cluj in Romania, Dallas in the USA, Mainz in Germany, Opole in Poland, Pécs in Hungary, Reggio Emilia in Italy, Skopje in Macedonia, Volgograd in the USSR, Białystok in Poland and York in the UK. Scarcely a week passed without a deputation from one of them paying a visit. Facing yet another mayoral reception, Kir saw he could promote both local winemakers and bottlers of *crème de cassis* if he combined their products in a drink to serve at such affairs.

Kir may be the perfect *aperitif*. It resembles a soft drink, but wine adds an element of sophistication. Best of all, as far as the French are concerned, it offers an opportunity to display discrimination, knowledge and intelligence – in other words, to show off.

For a start, it's chic to ask for Kir Royale, made with champagne. Even more obscurely, one can request Kir Cardinale (which uses red wine) or a Kir Communard, identical to the Cardinale, but named for the anarchists who briefly controlled Paris in 1871, and were, of course, Reds. Kir Bretagne uses cider, a major product of Brittany, while Kir Marcassin replaces wine with *marc de Bourgogne*, a rough brandy distilled from grape stems, seeds and skins.

The syrup can also vary: there's Kir *framboise*, with raspberry instead of blackcurrant, or Kir *pêche*, with peach syrup - pretty, if insipid. But Kir's most exotic variant was doomed never to be drunk by the celebrity for whom it was created. In 1960, Mayor Kir, learning that Russian premier Nikita Khrushchev would be visiting France for a summit meeting, invited

him to Dijon. In anticipation, he created Kir Double K: two shots of *crème de cassis*, four of Aligoté and four of vodka. But just before his arrival, CIA spy pilot Gary Powers was shot down over Soviet territory and the summit broke up amid mutual recriminations. Kir Double K became another victim of the Cold War.

THE SLICE OF LIFE

BREAD AND HISTORY

Bread has been important to the French since medieval times. It eked out the vegetable stew or *potage* on which the poor survived. Paintings of sixteenth-century country feasts show no meat or wine, just beer, soup and bread. Round, flat loaves, called 'trenchers', served as plates; a good eater is still called a trencherman. Meat was a luxury for the peasantry. When Henri IV came to the throne in 1589 and announced, 'If God spares me, I will make sure that no peasant in my realm will lack the means to have a fowl in his pot on Sunday,' it seemed like an impossible dream.

Even more than cheese and wine, bread is central to the French personality, a fact UNESCO recognized when it declared the *baguette* an item of Intangible Cultural Heritage in 2022. One of the greatest compliments is to say of someone, 'He is like good bread.' For centuries, bread signified the gulf between classes; the higher up the social ladder, the more finely milled your flour, and the whiter your bread. Of someone who succeeded early in life, then fell on hard times, it's said they 'ate their white bread first'.

Bread is less a food than a character, with a personality. One should never place bread on the table with the crust down. That shows disrespect. Some traditionalists cut a cross on the underside of each new loaf, a nod towards the biblical injunction to Adam and Eve, 'Thou shalt eat the herb of the field; in the sweat of thy face thou shalt eat bread.' Also, the *baguette* and its larger cousin, the *pain*, should never be sliced but always torn. This facilitates the function for which they're best suited: ripping off a chunk of bread to mop up the sauce.

To deny the people bread or to tamper with its quality is enough to bring down a government or dethrone a king. Until the Industrial Revolution, uprisings in Europe often began in the summer after a poor harvest. As the price of bread rose, the proletariat either raided the granaries or mobbed the palace. Bread, or its absence, sparked the French Revolution of 1789. In July 1788, hailstorms destroyed the harvest. The winter that followed froze canals and rivers, paralyzing the traffic of grain. Stored for too long in damp conditions, cereals spoil. Any flour made from them can appear yellow, smell bad and harbour the poisonous fungus ergot that caused St Anthony's Fire, a burning sensation in the limbs.

The cost of a 2-kg loaf of bread rose from 8 sous in the summer of 1787 to 12 sous by October 1788 and 15 sous by February 1789. At the time, a family of four needed two loaves a day to survive, but the average working man received only about 30 sous a day. Bakers adulterated wheat flour with cheaper grains, such as millet, and even sawdust. Barefoot mobs of Parisians walked the 27km to Versailles and gathered at the gates, demanding that the king open the royal granaries. As they walked, they chanted, 'We're going to see the baker, the baker's wife, and the little baker's boy.'

If the *sans culottes* expected sympathy, they were complaining in the wrong place. Aristocrats didn't eat bread. They preferred *brioche*, soft, white and rich in eggs and milk. According to legend, Marie Antoinette asked a lady-in-waiting what the protesters wanted. 'They say they have

no bread, madame,' she replied, to which the Queen is supposed to have responded, '*S'ils n'ont plus de pain, qu'ils mangent de la brioche*' (If they have no bread, then let them eat brioche). It's a good story, but untrue. When the story was first told (about someone else), Marie Antoinette was only ten years of age, and still at home in her native Austria, with no thought of ever living in France. The tale was later maliciously and incorrectly assigned to Marie Antoinette; as far as the revolutionaries who killed her were concerned, if she didn't say it, she *should* have.

Given the importance of bread, bakers enjoyed a degree of respect. A community could survive for days, even weeks without meat and even wine, but as the traditional *baguette*, made of flour, water, yeast and salt but no fat, became hard and inedible in twenty-four hours, a fresh loaf each day was essential. The well-being of the local baker was important. In one of its first reforms, the Commune rescinded a law that required bakers to work through the night. Letting them sleep until 4 a.m. improved their temper, and thus the quality of the bread.

But the French are changing their mind about bread. After a century of scorning American-style square sliced bread, known as *pain de mie* or 'crumb' bread, plastic-wrapped packs have appeared on most supermarket shelves, next to the robust country breads pioneered by the Parisian baker Lionel Poilâne in the 1930s and now manufactured by his daughter Apollonia. A slice of Poilâne's trademark loaf, the flattened cannonball of wholemeal sourdough known as a *boule* or *miche*, makes the perfect base for grilled cheese or *charcuterie*. The *baguette* itself has also diversified. The 400g *flute* is rivalled by the thinner 125g *ficelle* and the *tradition* or *rustique*, distinctively pointed at both ends, with a chewier crust and denser crumb.

Although France still consumes more than six billion *baguettes* annually, bakeries have been closing at the rate of 400 a year, shrinking from 55,000 in 1970 to 35,000 today. Some blame the cost of staff. The rules about what constitutes a true *baguette* are strict, and make production labour-intensive. Dough cannot be prepared ahead of time and frozen, a requirement that conflicts with modern working methods. Or is it that people just don't like bread as much as before? Could they be eating more cake?

IF THERE'S NO GOD,

WHO INVENTED CHOCOLATE?

That Paris has more and better chocolate shops than any city in the world is down to an oddity of social etiquette. Since the French rarely invite people into their homes, such a visit is a matter of some importance, and it's customary to take a small gift. Over time, the range of appropriate gifts has narrowed. To bring anything which the hosts might be expected to provide could be seen as a slur on their hospitality. Imagine guests turning up with their own cutlery, on the assumption that yours would not be good enough. Bringing an object for the home can mean that the guest may expect to see it on display on their next visit. Wine is the traditional gift in Anglo-Saxon countries but in Diane Johnson's novel *Le Divorce*, an American family's arrival with a bottle is greeted by their French host with a muttered, 'Didn't they think we'd give them a drink?'

The easiest option is flowers, particularly from a fashionable florist. *Which* florist can matter, however, and provident hostesses have been known to save the wrapping paper of a particularly chic one for later use on bouquets bought somewhere less expensive. But what else can one bring that the hosts would never create for themselves?

Well, chocolates, of course.

As the first chocolate to reach France from Mexico in the middle of the seventeenth century was reserved for royalty, it never lost its aura of luxury. Early descriptions classified it as a drug, recommended for 'vapours of the spleen'. In 1823, *chocolatier* Antoine Gallais advised that it was 'prescribed by doctors with great success in cases of colds, catarrh, angina and those irritations of the throat which have become so frequent at this time because of the continual changes in the atmosphere. Chocolate also makes the organs of breathing more supple, helps those recovering from gastritis, and from all afflictions caused by inflammation.'

Hot chocolate was the beverage one consumed before rising in the morning and the last thing before going to bed at night. (The chocolate placed on the pillow in some hotels is the last vestige of this practice.) The Marquise de Sévigné, a lady at the court of Louis XIV and a tireless letter writer, liked *chocolat chaud* so much that her young African servant brought her a pot in bed each morning and evening. She cut back after rumours of side-effects. 'But what do you have to say about chocolate?' she wrote to her

pregnant daughter in 1671. 'Are you not afraid of how it can burn the blood? What if all the effects that appear miraculous mask some sort of diabolical combustion? What do your doctors say? I loved chocolate, as you know. But I think it did burn me; and furthermore, I have heard many terrible stories about it. The Marquise de Coëtlogon drank so much chocolate when she was pregnant last year that she gave birth to a baby who was black as the devil, and died.'

Marie Antoinette can take some credit for making chocolate more accessible. In 1790, she asked the Versailles court pharmacist Sulpice Debauve to make some powdered medicine more palatable. He mixed it with cocoa, sugar and almond milk, and pressed the mixture into discs that resembled a Spanish gold coin, the *pistole*, each stamped with the *fleur-de-lys* emblem of the Bourbons – the original of today's boxed chocolate selections.

Luckier than his queen, Debauve survived the Revolution and launched his first shop in Paris in 1800. Shrewdly, he offered his expertise to Napoleon, who reconfirmed him as official *chocolatier* to the court. Debauve's nephew, Antoine Gallais, joined him in 1823, by which time Napoleon's own architects, Charles Percier and Pierre Fontaine, had designed the premises on rue des Saints-Pères. A gem of the Empire style in gilt and blue, it suited a city that saw itself as an imperial capital to rival ancient Athens or Rome.

The *chocolat chaud* enjoyed by the Marquise de Sévigné became a café staple. Marcel Proust and Coco Chanel drank theirs at Angelina on rue de Rivoli. It still uses chocolate from Niger, Ghana and Côte d'Ivoire. They add no water or milk. True hot *chocolate* and nothing else, it's so thick that it barely pours from the jug in which it's served.

Modern dieticians disparage chocolate, failing to take into account its power to solace and charm. 'Everywhere in the world,' says restaurateur Alain Ducasse (who markets his own line), 'there are tensions – economic, political, religious. So we need chocolate.' Marcel Proust concurred. 'I recommend,' he wrote to a friend, 'that you regularly taste the exquisite chocolates made by Debauve and Gallais as a way of never losing sight of the true meaning of life.'

LE BEAUJOLAIS NOUVEAU EST ARRIVÉ!
THE YEARLY RACE

Just as the reds and browns of autumn segue into the greys and black of winter, nature and the French capacity for enjoyment insert a colourful leaf into the calendar. All over France, bars and wine merchants, known as *cavistes* (because they possess cellars or *caves*) display posters announcing '*Le Beaujolais Nouveau est arrivé!*' (The new Beaujolais has arrived!).

Most French wines aren't varietal but regional, named for the district or *terroir* that produced them rather than the grape from which they were pressed. Forget Cabernet Sauvignon, Pinot Noir, Merlot and Chardonnay. Look instead for Bordeaux, Bourgogne, Côtes du Rhône, Champagne – and Beaujolais. Such labels are hard-won. Under the system of Appellation d'origine contrôlée (AOC), *viticulteurs* face heavy penalties if they label as Champagne a wine that hasn't been produced to the strict rules of *méthode champenoise* or claim Bordeaux status when their wine should be classed as Côtes de Blaye. A similar system protects certain cheeses, butters and meats, a reminder that France remains a farming nation, proud of its produce and quick to defend it. When a post-war communist regime was mooted, General de Gaulle dismissed the possibility, jeering, 'How can any one party govern a country with 246 varieties of cheese?' (He actually under-played it; there are closer to a thousand.)

Beaujolais lies southeast of Paris, just north of Lyon. The local Gamay grape bursts early and yields a light red wine which can be drunk after only a few months in the bottle – just the thing, locals decided, to lubricate their tonsils before they hunkered down for winter. Legally, no wine could be released so soon after bottling but the authorities made an exception. Other *terroirs* have to wait until 15 December if their wine is to qualify under Appellation contrôlée. Beaujolais alone can be sold earlier, from the third Thursday in November.

In the United States, Beaujolais Nouveau is promoted as a drink for Thanksgiving, which falls one week later. In the 1960s, delivery of the first bottles became a competition. Drivers were rewarded for being the first into Paris or London with the new vintage. Within a decade, such contests had gone international, with cases rushed across the Atlantic or the Pacific and delivered by private plane, racing car or even elephant. In Beaujolais itself, the arrival was an occasion for celebration. Over a hundred Beaujolais Nouveau-related festivals took place in the region. One of them, Les Sarmentelles, held in Beaujeu, the region's capital, lasted for days. The winner of the annual tasting contest won their weight in wine.

Is the Beaujolais Nouveau worth the fuss and its sometimes inflated price? 'The worst tastes like the saddest kind of cheap wine,' admitted one authority, 'thin and acidic, with a banana candy or bubble-gum vibe. The best thing about Beaujolais Nouveau is that it's made to drink *now*. You don't need any anxiety about keeping it, wondering if it will get better. It's not supposed to get better; drink it today.'

A declining market in wine has led to a succession of scandals. In the early 2000s, one of the most widely publicized swirled around collector and dealer Rudy Kurniawan and his passion for the Domaine de la Romanée-Conti, a 9-ha *terroir* in Burgundy that produces small quantities of a wine peerless in quality and correspondingly high in value. Kurniawan's connoisseurship earned him the nickname Doctor Conti and helped launch his career as a buyer and seller of the finest burgundies. His tastings of rare vintages attracted the wealthiest collectors. But in 2008 an American lawyer questioned the labels on a batch of bottles from the Clos Saint-Denis *terroir*, offered for sale by Kurniawan at around $500,000. Investigators raiding his home discovered a laboratory for blending rare old vintages with cheaper wines, as well as equipment to print fake labels. Kurniawan was convicted and imprisoned for ten years, and ordered to repay $28.4 million to his victims, but the world of wine would take many years to recover.

Not all frauds are so flamboyant. Appellation d'origine contrôlée limits the amount a producer can bottle. Any excess is sold off, to be repacked in cheap 3-litre boxes, or marketed by foreign supermarkets under their own brand. But what if you shipped a tanker or two of your excess to a more prestigious *terroir* which bottled it as its own? In 2017, major merchant Raphaël Michel was accused of mislabelling, over a four-year period, fifty million bottles of Côtes du Rhône as more expensive Châteauneuf-du-Pape.

News of these frauds warned wine drinkers to take more care with their purchases. This in turn boosted the popularity of tastings. *Cavistes* offer them, and tour companies sell sampling trips to Burgundy and Champagne. Under the veneer of scholarship, however, most conclude with an invitation to buy; sometimes just a bottle – but why not an entire case, shipped direct to your home? To make this outcome more likely, clients are coaxed to sample as many wines as possible, and in as many variants: the slope with the chalk, the dry year and the one in which it rained. But sampling is not the same as tasting. In tasting, one sniffs the wine, sips, appreciates it, then spits it out. With sampling, one still sniffs and sips, but then swallows, and probably takes another glass. A reputable *caviste* will provide a *crachoir* (spittoon). No *crachoir*? Drink on – but expect, at the end, to feel the effects in your head and your wallet.

Worldwide, the popularity of wine is plunging, even in France, as the popular taste turns more to beer. Domestic consumption is down 15 per cent and the government has allocated €200 million to destroy surplus stock and support producers. Wine will still be produced, but just for the alcohol, to be used in hand sanitizer, cleaning products and perfume. *Viticulteurs* are being encouraged to move into other areas, such as olives. According to the Minister for Agriculture, the industry needs to 'look to the future, think about consumer changes, and adapt'. French wine growers have faced disaster before – infestation of the *Phylloxera* mite, Nazi Occupation and, most recently, climate change – so this is nothing new. They will probably respond in the time-honoured way. Anybody seen the corkscrew?

WAITERS AND WAITING

'Rude waiters' are an aspect of Paris life about which visitors often complain, while 'stupid customers' loom large in the grumbles of those who wait tables. The conflict is probably insoluble. Waiters might be more patient if they were better recompensed in a chronically underpaid trade, while visitors who've contended with strange streets, sore feet and a raging thirst are disinclined to politeness when they desperately wish for a clean toilet and a stiff drink.

The chronic animosity towards waiters probably accounts for the relish with which citizens of Paris – and, increasingly, other cities – will gather to observe the wobbling progress of a short, balding man with an apologetic moustache and wearing a white cotton jacket as he weaves down a city street carrying, high on one palm, a metal tray supporting a tall bottle and two glasses. A few steps behind him trot dozens more, tall, short, young, old, but all similarly loaded and dressed. Crowds line the sidewalk, some cheering, many jeering. They are spectators at another event in the crowded social life of Paris, its annual *Course des garcons de café* (Waiters' race).

Dating back to the 1920s, the race celebrates the expertise of the city's waiters and waitresses. Competitors must carry a round metal tray on which sits a bottle and two full glasses, and spill not a drop. There are cities in which this would present no challenge to even the most preoccupied walker, but Paris is not among them. Road surfaces vary. Cobblestones from the days before Haussmann alternate with the granite cubes that replaced them, and areas where a layer of bitumen has shuffled all three surfaces into foot-tangling confusion. It only needs one competitor to stumble for a dozen runners to go down with them, arms flailing, in a confusion of curses, broken glass and rolling metal trays.

Traditionally, the race takes place in April but in some years it has formed part of the Bastille Day celebrations in July. It even continued during the German Occupation, a gesture of support for an industry that suffered from shortages of coffee, sugar and alcohol, not to mention the deportation of young Frenchmen. From 1970, waitresses were allowed to compete. By then, other cities in France and elsewhere had taken up the custom, only to see it falter, at least in Paris, around 2000, overwhelmed by the many other celebrations of the millennium. The race resumed in 2011 but, like many traditions, didn't survive the Covid-19 lockdowns.

Most French versions of the race stipulate a correct waiter uniform – white jacket, long apron or tail coat – and proof that the contestant is employed by a café or restaurant. Other countries admit competitors with suspect credentials and even in fancy dress. All, however, insist that the tray be held in one hand alone. The use of two hands is permitted only to steady items, and then for no more than three paces, while employing chewing gum to hold bottle and glass in place is strictly forbidden.

The Paris race usually commences in the Place de l'Opéra, under the benign domination of Garnier's opera house. The route winds through the city centre, passing the church of the Madeleine, transiting Place de la Concorde and continuing up the Champs-Élysée, before crossing the Seine next to the Eiffel Tower, following Boulevard Saint-Germain back across the river towards Notre-Dame and arriving at the Hôtel de Ville, where exhausted survivors stagger over the finishing line.

Such events help close the gap between waiter and customer which visitors in particular find difficult to bridge. Traditionally, servants were simply animate tools, with no personality of their own. One accorded them the same degree of care and attention as a hammer or a spade. But with the service economy, *les domestiques*, while still serving a useful purpose, became people too.

The contradictions of their role interested Jean-Paul Sartre. In his key existential text of 1943, *Being and Nothingness*, he used the degree of calculation required in waiting tables to comment on 'the ceremony of our daily lives'. To him, the comportment of a waiter was a kind of performance. 'Consider this boy,' he wrote. 'He's lively and alert, but a little too precise, a little too fast in the way he approaches his customers. He bows too quickly, and his voice and eyes express an interest in their order that's a touch too enthusiastic; his eyes somewhat too full of solicitude. When he returns, it's briskly but a little unsure, carrying his tray like a tightrope walker, perpetually unstable, with an awkwardness he corrects with a movement of his arm, a touch of his hand.'

How should we treat the people who provide us with food and drink? As servants? As a kind of friend? Sartre was right in seeing everything taking place in a café or restaurant as – like most kinds of human behaviour – a show. Why do waiters wear an apron or white jacket, unless as a kind of costume? Why does the owner stand alertly behind the bar, exchanging banalities with the customers and polishing the *zinc* that doesn't need polishing? As customers, we too have parts to play. They require us, on entering, to greet the host – '*Bonjour, m'sieur*', or, if his wife is there, '*Bonjour'sieur'dame*.' If other people are present, we include them too, with a general nod – fellow guests, whom we may get to know better in due course. We '*Bonjour*' the waiter as well, then let him take up the part in which he's been cast. And if the production has pleased us, we leave, as a kind of applause, the accolade of a generous tip.

HISTORY

THE HISTORY OF BASTILLE DAY

On 14 July each year, France celebrates its national festival, Bastille Day. Dignitaries fill stands erected along the Champs-Élysées and around Place de la Concorde. Contingents from the armed services parade as aircraft roar overhead. At night, the sky fills with fireworks – state-provided, although it's traditional for citizens to explode a few of their own Roman candles and cherry bombs.

Some spectators may recall that, beneath their feet, Louis XVI, as well as most of the royal family and its court, were guillotined, along with many thousand others. Blood soaking into the stones of what was then Place de la Revolution created such a stench that for years even dogs wouldn't approach.

It's not this aspect of the Revolution that *quatorze juillet* celebrates, but rather the day when the Paris mob, having failed to attract the attention of Louis XVI to a national shortage of grain, among other deficiencies of his reign, attacked the most convenient symbol of his power, the Bastille. Once part of the fortifications protecting Paris, it had become a prison for political opponents of the king and others incarcerated 'at his majesty's pleasure'. The mob that broke down its doors was less concerned with releasing prisoners than with the gunpowder and weapons they hoped to find inside. Disappointed at discovering nothing, they slaughtered the prison governor and most of his staff.

As much as one might wish that hundreds of grateful radicals had stumbled into the sunshine and the arms of waiting friends, only seven men remained in the Bastille, none with much in the way of a political pedigree. After the publication of some embarrassing memoirs by former inmates, the crown had downgraded the status of the Bastille and relocated the prisoners elsewhere. One of them was Donatien, Marquis de Sade, who'd been locked up because his family begged the king to get him off the streets and stop embarrassing them with his outrageous fantasies. The marquis didn't waste his time in prison. By stitching together smuggled sheets of paper, he'd completed most of a sprawling catalogue of cruelty called *The 120 Days of Sodom*, but been forced to leave the manuscript behind. It's said he 'wept blood' at having to abandon his masterwork, written in a minuscule hand and rolled into a bulky scroll. But friends retrieved it, leading to its reconstruction and publication in 1904.

The Revolution of 1789 was entirely in character for a nation where political progress – which, in most countries, occurs in an orderly manner: debate, followed by elections, with the occasional ripple of a scandal – takes place in fits and starts, with periods of grumbling tranquillity interrupted by outbreaks of violence and disorder. After 1789, there was the *coup d'état* of 1801 that put Napoleon I on the throne, his forced abdication in 1814, the July Uprising of 1832 (that's the one in *Les Misérables),* the Napoleonic restoration of 1848 and the anarchist Commune of 1871, leading in time to *les evenements* of 1968.

Not that the population in general hopes for a revolution. If and when it comes, past experience suggests only a handful will actively participate. But the rest won't interfere. Even when Germany occupied France between 1940 and 1944, almost nobody resisted. Could it be that France, a rural country – the same population as Britain but five times the area – is ruled by the seasonality that dominates life on the land?

Once the Revolution gave a voice to landowners and farmers, support grew for a calendar that reflected the rural nature of French life. Nobody foresaw the chaos it would cause. The Republican Calendar was as uncompromising as the guillotine. In accordance with the new decimal system of measurement, each day was divided into ten hours, and each hour into one hundred minutes. The twelve months each contained three ten-day weeks, called *décades*. The tenth day of each week, Décadi, replaced Sunday as the day of rest.

Instead of names taken from mythology, the months were given new ones that evoked the season. Fructidor was the month of fruit, Floreal the month of flowers, Thermidor the month of heat. The man responsible for this creation, Fabre d'Églantine, went to the guillotine before it could be fully implemented, and Napoleon I, when he came to power, decided there were more pressing matters, and returned to the old system. All the same, the idea had merit. Ecclesiastes 3:1–8 suggests that 'For everything there is a season, and a time for every matter under heaven …' including 'a time to love, and a time to hate; a time for war, and a time for peace'. Maybe the French farmer knew something the revolutionaries did not.

TO LIVE AND DIE BY THE SWORD
DUELLING AND DUELLISTS

The great French historical novels are among the most durable of romances, as exciting today as when they were written two centuries ago. Every few decades, some filmmaker revisits *The Three Musketeers*, *The Hunchback of Notre-Dame*, *The Count of Monte Cristo*, *Cyrano de Bergerac* or *The Man in the Iron Mask*. The swirl of the cape, the flash of steel, the courtly bow, the heroine's face turned away in terror ... all these have a lasting appeal.

The Olympic fencing competitions offer a reminder of those exciting times, if a pale one. Masks, protective clothing, buttons on the foils and sabres with blunted blades remove the original point of duelling – to injure or kill an opponent. To the duellists of the past, honour was not satisfied unless each person exposed themselves to the greatest degree of risk, and a clash only ended when blood was spilt. It was usual to expose as much vulnerable skin as possible. Some even tore off the shirt sleeves. This was done in the interests of freedom of movement but, particularly in Germany, the less protection meant the greater chance of a glamorous scar. For a wound to be truly honourable, it must have been inflicted in an affair of honour and by a person of status.

Each new ruler of France sternly forbade duelling but knew the custom would never be stamped out as long as swordsmen enjoyed it so much. Like western gunfighters, the best of them lived off their prowess, competing with themselves until somebody more expert put an end to their careers. Ambitious newcomers trailed the great duellists, often acting as their seconds, and frequently getting involved in the action with other seconds, until a duel became a brawl.

Anywhere one goes in old Paris, there are reminders. Most duels took place in wooded areas where they wouldn't attract attention. Many chose Le Pré aux Clercs (The Field of the Clerks), a meadow on the left bank of the Seine, on the site now occupied by Quai Malaquais, but the preferred venue was the gardens behind the Palais du Luxembourg. In those days neglected and overgrown, it provided cover for dire deeds of every persuasion.

The Dumas, *père* and *fils*, as well as most historical novelists, based their stories on actual people. From *The Three Musketeers*, the real D'Artagnan lived on what is now rue Servandoni, Athos on rue Ferou, Aramis on rue de Vaugirard, all within a short walk of the Jardin du Luxembourg. Savinien de Cyrano de Bergerac also existed, and was rejected by women and mocked by men on account of an enormous proboscis. As a rule, the French don't mock big noses. A common facial type features an organ so prominent that people say '*Il peut fumer sous la douche*' (He could smoke a cigarette under the shower). But Bergerac was not one to take a joke. His skill with both sword and words made him famous, and inspired Edmond Rostand to write his 1897 play, a star vehicle for generations of actors.

One of the best novels in the genre known as *cap et épée* (cloak and dagger) is barely known outside France, since its plot is so uniquely French. *Le Bossu* (literally 'The Hunchback' but retitled *En Garde* in English) appeared in 1857 from one of the rivals of Alexandre Dumas *père*, Paul Féval. It depends on the fact that the French traditionally regard sufferers

from kyphosis and other spinal deformations as lucky with money. Until recently, victims loitered outside casinos, selling to gamblers the opportunity to rub their back for luck. Financiers employed them as financial advisers, a loophole exploited by the protagonist of *Le Bossu* to infiltrate the villain's inner circle.

Le Bossu anticipates *Cyrano de Bergerac* in having a hero who makes creative use of a disability, if a faked one. The main characters are the dashing Duke de Nevers and young mercenary Henri de Lagardère. Each new duke in the Nevers line is taught the Nevers thrust, a tricky piece of swordplay that kills unfailingly with a point between the eyes. Lagardère, hoping to learn its secret, waylays the duke as he returns to Paris with his infant daughter Aurore, and is about to challenge him when they are attacked by thugs hired by Nevers' evil cousin Gonzague. Lagardère sides with Nevers and drives them off. The duke is fatally wounded, but entrusts his new friend with Aurore and the secret of the Thrust. Years later, Lagardère, disguised as a *bossu*, infiltrates Gonzague's business and wrecks it before killing him in a duel with – of course – the Nevers Thrust.

Féval obviously learned from *Notre-Dame de Paris*, since he sets some scenes in the Cour des miracles, that corner of the Marais, also described by Hugo, where, at the end of a day's begging, the missing limbs of the mutilated miraculously reappear and the apparently blind regain their sight. The financial background is also accurate. The Revolution of 1789 outlawed trading in shares but until then certain streets were Paris's stock exchanges. In disguise, Lagardère sidles among the speculators, murmuring the few incendiary words that will ignite a panic and ruin Gonzague. In foreseeing a world where assassins kill with numbers, and the pen – or at least a spreadsheet – is mightier than the sword, *Le Bossu* was truly prescient.

THE 1871 COMMUNE

Most visitors to Paris know about the Revolution of 1789. Some have even heard about the July Uprising of 1832 (the one in *Les Misérables*). But any mention of the Commune of 1871 generally produces blank looks – even though some of what took place in its turbulent few months had far-reaching effects.

In 1870, Napoleon III went to war with Prussia. The Prussians won every battle and besieged Paris, bombarding its suburbs to rubble. From Tours, where it had fled, the government negotiated a peace, including the emperor's immediate abdication. The Prussians announced a victory parade through the city. With the French army having retreated in disorder to Versailles, Parisians, convinced they would be slaughtered, raised the money to buy 400 cannon, placed them on the hill of Montmartre – a bastion of left-wing activism – and prepared to fight. The National Guard of 24,000 men swelled to 350,000 as the Prussians approached. But the parade was an anti-climax. The invaders behaved with decorum, then returned home. Paris found itself a free city of ordinary working men and women with the arms to defend itself.

On 18 March, the army belatedly reformed, and troops commanded by generals Claude Martin Lecomte and Jacques Leonard Clement-Thomas arrived to re-occupy Montmartre and seize its artillery. As they did so, a crowd of women, led by Louise Michel, an anarchist schoolteacher known as the Red Virgin of Montmartre ('red' because of her left-wing politics), blocked them. The generals ordered the soldiers to fire on the protestors, but most were Parisians, and refused. Siding with the National Guard, they imprisoned their astonished commanders. As the remainder of the army retreated in confusion, suppressed resentments among the mutineers, fanned by anarchist radicals, erupted in a murderous impulse to revenge themselves on their former officers. 'Soldiers broke the windows of the room where General Lecomte was confined,' wrote one witness, 'threw themselves upon him, dragging him towards the garden. This man who, in the morning, had three times given the order to fire upon the people, wept, begged for pity, and spoke of his family. He was forced against the wall and fell under the bullets.' They shot Clément-Thomas shortly after.

Stunned by the speed of events, the rebels hesitated. Some occupied the Hôtel de Ville, the city's town hall. 'That evening we did not know what to do,' recalled one. 'We did not want possession of the Hôtel de Ville. We were very embarrassed by our authority.' Anarchists, Marxists and republicans bickered. Some favoured attacking the demoralized army, but moderates prevailed, electing a Communal Council to run the free city.

The ninety-two-member council focused on practicalities. To re-start the economy, communards forced money-lenders to return tools pawned by craftsmen. Where the owners of a business had fled or died, workers were encouraged to take over. All debt was suspended for ninety days at zero interest. Bakers were no longer forced to work all night so that Parisians could have fresh morning *baguettes*. Free soup kitchens, called *marmites*, were set up. Women on the council demanded the right to vote and an end to prostitution, as well as the recognition of common-law marriages and illegitimate children. Widows of National Guardsmen killed in the fighting received pensions. The Catholic church, always supportive of the state, became a target. Its property was seized, including schools, in which a non-religious curriculum was introduced. Churches were allowed to remain open only if citizens could also use them for political meetings.

The painter Gustave Courbet was placed in charge of museums and art galleries. His credentials, both artistic and political, were impeccable. Before the war, Napoleon III offered him membership of the Légion d'honneur. He refused. 'When I am dead,' he announced, 'let this be said of me: "He belonged to no school, to no church, to no institution, to no academy, least of all to any regime except the regime of liberty."' For the first time, the art of the Louvre, until then reserved for royal eyes, could be enjoyed by everyone. Concerts and performances of opera and theatre took place outdoors, and for free. Communards danced in the streets and sang '*Les Temps de Cerises*' (The Time of Cherries), a song that became an anthem of the uprising.

Not all the anarchists approved of this workers' paradise. Radicals, determined to erase all vestiges of the former royalist government, took hostages, including the Archbishop of Paris and, when the government refused to release political prisoners, killed them. Female arsonists, called *petroleuses*, roamed the city, destroying any building associated with the hated emperor. They torched the Tuileries Palace, the Ministry of Finance, the Council of State, the Palace of the Legion d'honneur, the High Court, even the Hôtel de Ville, seat of what passed for a communard administration. The Hôtel de Ville survived but the Tuileries Palace burned for two days. When the arsonists tried to also burn the Louvre, Courbet

intervened. Seeing they were bent on destroying something, he suggested the stone column on Place Vendôme. Built by Napoleon I to celebrate his victories, it was covered in sculpted bronze plates cast from the cannon of armies he'd defeated. They gleefully demolished it and the Louvre was saved.

This honeymoon couldn't last. Busy with reform and revenge, the communards didn't notice the army regrouping. When General Patrice de MacMahon, Duke of Magenta, marched to retake the city, they improvised barricades from the rubble of buildings demolished by the Prussians and prepared to fight. But amateurs were no match for de MacMahon's troops, most of whom, imported from the south, felt no loyalty to Parisians. The surviving communards took refuge in the gypsum mines that honeycombed Montmartre. However, the army, guided by a traitor, blew up the tunnels and forced them back to the surface. By the end of May, the last had surrendered or fled.

In what became known as *la semaine sanglante* (Bloody Week), thousands were executed in the Jardin du Luxembourg and at Cimetière du Père-Lachaise. Of the 12,500 who survived to be tried, about 10,000 were convicted, mostly on little evidence or none at all. 'In Paris, everyone is guilty!' a prosecutor snarled. Twenty-three were legally executed and about 7,500 jailed. Others, including Louise Michel, were deported to New Caledonia, a territory in the South Pacific.

Paris remained under martial law for five years as a new regime rooted out the last dissidents. But the spirit of the Commune survived. It helped inspire the 1917 Russian Revolution. The anthem of international Socialism, the 'Internationale', was written by a communard. Its first lines – 'Arise, you prisoners of starvation/ Arise, you wretched of the earth' – were known to every communist.

At Père-Lachaise, a sculpture marks the Mur des Fédérés, where 147 men and women were shot on 28 May 1871 and buried in a common grave. The Hôtel de Ville and other targets of arson were restored. After much discussion, the burned-out shell of the Tuileries Palace was demolished, leaving only its Orangerie, the *jeu de paume* (real tennis) court, and the triumphal arch standing at the former entrance. The bronze plates of the Vendôme column were saved and the column rebuilt. Courbet was jailed for six months for his part in its demolition, fined 500 francs, and forced to pay for its restoration, at the rate of 10,000 francs a year. He died at the age of ninety-one in December 1877, a day before the final instalment was due. The church collected money by public subscription to construct the Basilica of Sacré-Coeur on the summit of Montmartre, above the mines where the last anarchists took refuge – not to commemorate them and the other victims of the Commune but to 'expiate the sins of the communards' in defying the church and executing its archbishop.

Louise Michel survived transportation and returned to France in 1880 a heroine. The black flag she carried is now the universal symbol waved by anarchists around the world. In 2004, the terrace in front of the cathedral became Square Louise Michel, and in 2020 the British artist Banksy funded a boat to rescue asylum seekers crossing the Mediterranean and named it for her.

EVERYBODY OUGHT TO HAVE A MAID
DOMESTIC LABOUR AND THE FEMME DE MÉNAGE

If a maid walks into her employer's bedroom without knocking, she shouldn't be surprised at what she sees, but the sight that confronts Célestine, heroine of Octave Mirbeau's 1900 novel *The Diary of a Chambermaid*, shocks even her: 'Monsieur was dead! Stretched on his back, in the middle of the bed, he lay with all the rigidity of a corpse. ... And I should have thought him asleep, if his face had not been violet, frightfully violet, the sinister violet of egg-plants. And ... Monsieur held, pressed between his teeth, one of my shoes, so firmly pressing it between his teeth that, after useless and horrible efforts, I was obliged to cut the leather with a razor, in order to tear it from him.'

A shoe fetishist for an employer wasn't typical of the problems facing domestic servants in *fin de siècle* Paris, but tyrannical employers and sexual advances came with the territory. Mirbeau claimed he wrote *The Diary of a Chambermaid* to expose the plight of women, who, in extreme cases, were preyed on by employment agencies and brutalized by employers. Nothing was cheaper than domestic labour. Women, fed up with life on the farm, fled to the cities, where those who didn't find work in a factory or in the sex trade fell back of cooking, cleaning and minding children; the very things they left home to avoid.

In this buyers' market, women worked simply for enough to eat and a place to sleep. Even Ernest and Hadley Hemingway, when they lived in a two-room fourth-floor cold-water flat in Paris with no lavatory, could afford a *femme de ménage*. Her name was Marie Rohrbach. She walked to their apartment each morning, prepared their meals, did the shopping, scrubbed their floors, took their clothes down to the Seine, washed them on one of the floating laundries known as *bateaux lavoirs*, ironed them, then returned home to her husband, a retired army man, to do the same chores. When the Hemingways' son John (aka Bumby) arrived, she became his nanny, often taking him to her family home in Brittany when his parents left Paris for weeks to ski or run with the bulls in Pamplona. Later, John confessed he saw more of her than he did of them. In old age, Marie had both legs amputated – the result, Hadley believed, of the grinding work she did for them over the years. She isn't mentioned in *A Moveable Feast* (1964), though in a deleted passage Hemingway does grumble about the high cost of keeping her on.

As a schoolboy, Octave Mirbeau was raped by the Jesuit priests charged with his education. He grew up close-lipped, irascible, embittered, plagued by clinical depression. 'The universe,' he wrote, 'appears to me like an immense, inexorable torture garden. Passions, greed, hatred, and lies; law, social institutions, justice, love, glory, heroism, and religion: these are its monstrous flowers and its hideous instruments of eternal human suffering.'

Given these views, it's not surprising he embraced anarchism. He did so despite the fact that, as a businessman and investor, as well as a journalist, novelist and dramatist, he was extremely rich. Paradoxically, his wealth made him an effective champion of the renegade and underdog. He defended Vincent van Gogh and Auguste Rodin against censorship and censure. When Alfred Dreyfus, a Jewish officer in the Army, was wrongly convicted of treason in 1894 and shipped to Devil's Island, Mirbeau's friend, the novelist Émile Zola, publicized the scandal in broadsides like the famous *J'Accuse*. Mirbeau's fortune funded the campaign that cleared Dreyfus's name and unmasked the real traitor, an aristocratic member of the military elite.

Célestine, the protagonist of *The Diary of a Chambermaid*, uses beauty and intelligence to advance herself at the expense of her bourgeois employers. In each new household, she spreads chaos. Her cheeky manner and voluptuous body reduce middle-aged businessmen to stammering idiocy. Their wives invite her into their boudoirs, supposedly to help them dress but actually to make lesbian overtures, and their sons beg her to initiate them into sex. As she acquiesces to some and refuses others, her fellow domestics watch from the shadows, sniggering at the stupidity of their 'betters'.

Her employers speak freely in front of her, allowing us to eavesdrop on some outrageous conversations:

> One day, I found [Madame] in her boudoir with a friend, describing how, with Monsieur, she'd visited a brothel where they'd watched two little hunchbacks having sex. 'You should see them, my dear,' I overheard Madame say. 'Nothing's more exciting.'

The same lady travels with a dildo, locked in a special velvet 'jewel case'. When a Customs Officer demands she open it for inspection, the woman is mortified, but suggests to Célestine that, if this happens again, the maid should claim ownership. 'Thanks very much, Madame,' she responds frostily, 'but when it comes to those sort of "jewels", I prefer them the way nature created them.'

Sexually active since the age of ten, Célestine easily outdoes her employers in perversity. Hired to nurse a young man in the last stages of tuberculosis, she not only gives into his pleas that she have sex with him before he dies but is aroused by the proximity of death to a sadomasochistic frenzy. After the boy dies in her arms, blood-spattered but satiated, Célestine moves on to a house which harbours a cache of pornography, which she devours.

By the time she arrives at the château where most of the story is set, Célestine is more than ready for them. Playing her employers and their neighbours off against one another, she soon has them panting for her favours, which she coolly withholds until one of her suitors offers marriage. In an irony that may have influenced D.H. Lawrence when he wrote *Lady Chatterley's Lover*, she chooses the hulking gamekeeper, Joseph, a virulent antisemite, sadist and, possibly, sexual murderer. But in him Célestine recognizes something of her own perverse, erotic nature. Joseph burgles his employers' house to steal their silver, and uses the money to buy a bar in a seaside town. Joseph and Célestine marry, and prosper. There's no concluding moral to the story, just a total acceptance of her new life. 'Really I am powerless against Joseph's will. [He] holds me, possesses me, like a demon. And I'm happy in being his. I feel that I shall do whatever he wishes me to do, and that I shall go wherever he tells me to go ... Even to crime!'

As *The Diary of a Chambermaid* illustrates, sex between employee and servant was common. Ernest Hemingway had an affair with the young concierge in the building where he completed *The Sun Also Rises*. Genuine rapport or mutual respect, however, were rare. An exception was the relationship between Marcel Proust and his housekeeper, Céleste Albaret. An uneducated girl from the country, married to his chauffeur Odilon, she charmed Proust with her naiveté – he had to explain that 'Napoleon' and 'Bonaparte' were the same person – and earned his confidence with her fierce protection of his privacy and care for his frail health. She was the only person he trusted with the manuscript of his epic novel cycle *À la recherche du temps perdu*. She adjusted to his day-for-night regime, accepted uncritically his homosexuality, neglected her own marriage to accommodate him, and remained with him until his death. Proust had told her, 'It is your beautiful little hands that will close my eyes.' To do so was her last act for the man she had come to love.

THE 1924 OLYMPICS

After the disastrous 1900 Olympic Games in Paris, marred by squabbling between rival ruling bodies, flagrant cheating and an eccentric choice of sports – croquet, balloon racing, pigeon-shooting with live pigeons – Baron Pierre de Coubertin hoped that the 1924 Olympiad, his last, would redeem the reputation of his home city. Amsterdam had already been chosen as the host, but he persuaded the committee to give Paris another chance.

The Olympics and rugby football have a long association. The game was invented at Rugby School, Warwickshire, UK, the innovative headmaster of which, Thomas Arnold, was a friend of Baron de Coubertin and influenced his decision to revive the Olympiad. Rugby is hard, tough and dirty, a reputation its players often seem intent on maintaining. Injuries are the badge of courage. Missing front teeth are common; likewise cauliflower ears, bandaged joints and surgical scars.

The New Zealand All Blacks precede each match with the *haka*, their version of a Māori war dance in which, to terrify their enemies, tribesmen stamped, shouted and grimaced. From the moment rugby became popular in France, it had an edge of violence. According to a history of the French sport, 'the game has been associated with the small towns of the south-west and their long history of resistance to centralization. Racism and sexism flourish, encouraged by symbolic boundaries and the myths of belonging to an imaginary community.'

The Olympics admitted rugby as a sport at the 1900 Paris Games, when a local team won gold. In 1920 the French took gold again, and were widely tipped to win in 1924. Not for the last time, however, politics intervened, leading to one of the Olympics' most disreputable incidents.

Since the armistice of 1918, France had struggled to extract from a bankrupt Germany the reparations promised as the price of peace. In particular, it demanded the return of the border region of Alsace-Lorraine, lost in the Franco-Prussian War of 1870–71 but ceded back under the Treaty of Versailles. In 1923, frustrated by the slow progress of the transfer, France sent troops into Alsace to seize the factories and mines of its richest region, the Ruhr. Britain and the United States brokered a compromise which required France to withdraw and accept reduced repayments. Feeling cheated, the French dragged their feet, which brought, just before the Games began in July 1924, a rebuke from the American government.

This was the climate in which American athletes, including its rugby team, arrived in Paris. French officialdom neglected no opportunity to show its displeasure. The players' luggage was searched minutely by customs, and items stolen. They were given misleading directions to the Olympic village, the first time this amenity was provided, and were denied the chance to practise. Parisians spat at them in the street.

Tensions increased as the rugby final approached between France and the United States. Fifty thousand spectators filled the Stade de Colombes, recently upgraded with new stands and metal barriers to prevent spectators from invading the pitch. From the start it was a grudge match. Fights broke out in the crowd and American supporters, outnumbered, were badly beaten. The match was delayed as the crowd, silent, watched the battered and bloodied victims passed over their heads to ambulances.

Within minutes of the game starting again, the French captain was carried off with a broken nose. Disquiet increased in the crowd as the American team ran rings around its opponents. Had there been no barriers, the match, which America won 17–3, might have ended in a riot. As it was, an uproar marred the medal ceremony. Catcalls drowned out the 'Star-Spangled Banner' and the Americans were forced to flee through an escape tunnel, pursued by an angry crowd. Rugby disappeared as an Olympic event after this *débacle*, but made a comeback of sorts at the 2016 Rio Games in a modified seven-a-side form. Future matches will take place, one hopes, without a repetition of the bloody clash of a century ago.

FEY AND DRUNKEN

RAYMOND AND ISADORA DUNCAN

From the moment in 1898 when their parents brought them from San Francisco to Europe, Isadora Duncan and her older brother Raymond recognized Paris as their spiritual home. Isadora was still a virgin when she met one of her idols, sculptor Auguste Rodin. Heavily bearded, in a monk-like robe, he was every inch the great artist. 'He gazed at me with lowered lids, his eyes blazing,' she recalled. 'He ran his hands over my neck, breast, stroked my arms and ran his hands over my hips, my bare legs and feet. He began to knead my whole body as if it were clay.' Having memorized her dimensions, Rodin was anxious to explore further, but Isadora fended him off, to her everlasting regret. To have lost her virginity to Rodin! What a start to her career.

After that, she devoted her life to dance. Touring Europe with her troupe, the Isadorables, she became so notorious for wild behaviour, both on stage and off, that Dorothy Parker nicknamed her 'Duncan Disorderly'. Raymond, meanwhile, fell in love with ancient Greece, adopting its lifestyle and wardrobe. Author John Glassco called him 'a walking absurdity who dressed in an ancient hand-woven Greek costume and wore his hair in long braids reaching to his waist, adding, on ceremonial occasions, a filet of bay leaves'.

Raymond started a commune on the edge of the Bois de Boulogne, where he aimed to replicate life in ancient Greece. Once he announced that unwed mothers, disowned by their families, would be welcome in his community, a number of them moved in, leaving their children to be raised communally while they crafted sandals and woven objects for sale. During the First World War, he visited convalescent hospitals and taught weaving to wounded soldiers. He also showed housewives how to spin knitting yarn from the raw wool with which most mattresses were stuffed.

In 1919, a building at 31 rue de Seine, in the heart of Saint-Germain-des-Prés, became, according to a sign above the columned entrance, the Akademia Raymond Duncan, identified modestly as 'The Artistic Centre of Paris'. A shop sold sandals, togas and scarves made at the commune. The Akademia also had a theatre, but with couches, not seats, where the audience, reclining, could endure, in considerable discomfort, Duncan's translations of Greek drama.

Meanwhile, Isadora continued to lead the émigré community in alcoholic misbehaviour, partying, as she danced, in a minimum of clothing. Novelist Michel Georges-Michel described one of her parties at which, reclining in Roman fashion, she 'poured out champagne from an immense amphora of jade to all those who reached up with their cups. She let down her hair, loosened her clothing, and asked everybody to follow her example. "It is as indecent to be dressed when the company is nude as to be sober when everybody is drunk".' She died violently in 1927, yanked by the neck onto a street in Nice as her trailing scarf caught in a wheel of the car rushing her to the bed of a new lover. She could not have wished for a more characteristic end.

During the 1930s, Raymond toured the USA, presenting his versions of Greek drama and giving interviews in which, reclining, as usual, he 'discoursed', wrote one disgruntled journalist, 'about the lack of art among us provincials'. E.B. White of the *New Yorker* mocked him in verse. 'To tend young goats on Attic hills/ And weave with Raymond Duncan/ I'm sure would aggravate my ills/ And make me fey and drunken.' Refusing to leave Paris during the Second World War, Duncan was among the first to welcome the allies in 1944. Although almost eighty, he hoisted the Stars and Stripes over the American Embassy and, according to one report, 'sang "Yankee Doodle Dandy" until he was hoarse'. But a post-war Saint-Germain-des-Prés preoccupied with existentialism had no time for the aesthetics of ancient Athens. 'Duncan followers are mainly aging maiden ladies,' wrote a reporter in 1949. 'They foregather at the Akademia every Saturday afternoon when the Master presents the "Stars of Paris," usually young artists or writers who read their own work or play the piano with concentrated fervour. The Master writes poetry himself and recites it at every opportunity.'

Duncan died aged ninety-one in 1966, the last of Saint-Germain's bohemians. At 31 rue de Seine, now turned into apartments, a plaque above the front door announces: '*George Sand (1804–1876) habita cette maison en 1831 puis Raymond Duncan y créa l'Academie de 1929 à 1966*'. Nothing remains of the shop, nor the workshop that used to occupy the entire ground floor. However, propped up against the inner courtyard wall are four carved stone reliefs from his workshop. In one, a man plucks at a lyre, watched quizzically by a goat. Others show potters moulding clay and men using sledgehammers to split stone. As it's unlikely the present tenants know anything of Raymond Duncan, the Akademia or his commune, these slabs belong to a past as remote as the ancient Greece that inspired them.

ERNEST HEMINGWAY
THE TELLER OR THE TALE?

T
hanks to a 2021 television documentary series, anyone who didn't know the legend of Ernest Hemingway is now fully acquainted with his story. It's a touchstone for any artist who dreams of finding fame and love in a foreign land.

We hardly need reminding of the stages in young Hemingway's involvement with the French capital. Limping from wounds won in battle, he arrived with his new wife in 1921, charmed the expatriate community – particularly Sylvia Beach, proprietor of the Shakespeare and Company bookshop and the barman at the Hôtel Ritz – wrote a bestseller, achieved international fame, relocated to Key West, Florida, in 1928, before returning to Paris in 1944 to 'liberate' both Beach and the Ritz, and then immortalizing his devotion in a posthumous memoir of the days when he was 'poor but happy in Paris'.

It's a story almost too good to be true. Perhaps because it mostly isn't.

Leaving aside his meagre war record – he handed out chocolate and cigarettes, but never fired a shot – and the shabby treatment of his first wife, married on the rebound from an unhappy love affair and dumped, along with his baby son, in favour of someone younger and richer, Hemingway had little good to say about Paris when he lived there, sneering at the 'semites' and 'ladies of all sexes' who patronized Montparnasse's cafés – comparing the mixture of languages in one of them, the Rotonde, to the twittering and squawking in the bird house at the zoo.

Scathing about fellow members of the 'lost generation', he sniped in words at his sometime mentor Gertrude Stein, and used his fists in an attempt to dominate such early supporters as Ezra Pound and Morley Callaghan. 'I thought he was a bully,' recalled theatrical caricaturist Al Hirschfeld. 'There was a little gym where a lot of the artists and writers used to come, and Hemingway was there and he was boxing all the time. And he would always pick some fellow about half his size and knock him down. He was a kind of sadist in many ways, I thought. I never saw him box anybody his own size.' He even wore out his welcome with Montmartre club owner Ada Smith (aka Bricktop, nicknamed so because of her red hair), who was used to dealing with the curdled cream of *bohème*. 'A lot of people were raving about him,' said Smith, 'but I never took to him. He just wanted to bring people down, and he had a way of doing it, and he was liable to punch you at the same time.'

Those who knew him in his later Paris years paint an equally unflattering picture of a gifted man ruined by self-indulgence. One remembered him as 'still the great literatus, but increasingly lushed to bits and surrounded by nobodies and even, sometimes, Parisians. A tab accompanied each drink and in due course they would all find their way across to Hemingway's area of table. By the end of a stint, he'd often have fifty or sixty under his chin. Before his eyes finally glazed over, he would pay them all and stumble out.'

Of Hemingway in his prime, the 'splendidly built young man with a torso of dazzling white' described by Wyndham Lewis, there was no sign – not, at least, until *A Moveable Feast* (1964) emerged three years after his death. For this, we can thank his widow Mary, who assembled his notes and chose the name. As seamlessly crafted as a cenotaph, *A Moveable Feast* enshrined for all time a vision of prelapsarian Paris and the giants who bestrode it.

Such was its effectiveness, however, that, for better or worse, it's this Paris and this Hemingway visitors want. Admirers flock to such historic sites as Shakespeare and Company and the Hemingway Bar at the Ritz, where a barman is eager to whip up his favourite martini, a potent mix of one part of vermouth to seventeen parts gin. The crowds who queue at Shakespeare and Company don't care that this isn't the shop Hemingway knew, and that it didn't even exist until 1962, when bookseller George Whitman acquired the name after the death of Sylvia Beach. As for the Ritz, its Hemingway Bar was one Paris watering hole where Ernie never raised a glass. Gossip having embedded in history the legend of him 'liberating the Ritz' in 1944, the management, after closing its former Women's Bar, to which females had been exiled in less enlightened times, decided in 1994 to redecorate it as a shrine to him.

Does anything remain of the Paris Hemingway really knew?

One can still visit the original premises of Shakespeare and Company at 12 rue de l'Odéon, a few doors down the street from where Sylvia and her companion, Adrienne Monnier, shared an apartment. Although a plaque, erected by the city, marks the site of Monnier's former shop – the Maison des Amis des Livres – diagonally opposite, Beach's shop has to make do with a miniscule tribute, just below the windows of the tiny upstairs apartment where she died, and where her body lay for some days, undiscovered. (An unofficial plaque noting that James Joyce's *Ulysses* was published here owes its existence to the James Joyce Society of Sweden and Finland.)

The closing of the original Shakespeare and Company in 1940, when Germany invaded, marked the last use of these premises as a bookshop. Shuttered for many years, it has been a Chinese gift store, a jeweller and, at the time of writing, a dress shop, although the present owner, aware of the site's literary significance, keeps a shelf of related books, and retails T-shirts and tote bags with a photograph of Beach and Joyce standing at either side of the shop entrance.

Hemingway's preferred hangout, the Closerie des Lilas, is still in business, though now, in common with most Paris cafés, a restaurant. A brass plate in its bar indicates where he occasionally held court. One more location deserves a mention. After working all morning in the Closerie, Hemingway sometimes walked down Boulevard de Montparnasse to where the Rotonde and Café du Dôme flank the intersection with Boulevard Raspail. When he first moved to Montparnasse, he patronized the Dôme but, as tourists increasingly overran it, preferred the unassuming Falstaff or Dingo, neighbourhood bars on the thoroughfare behind the boulevard that August Strindberg called 'dark and quiet rue Delambre, a street that more than any other in the neighborhood can make you miserable'.

Once a plain wooden-floored working-men's bistro, the Dingo became a clubhouse for expatriates after the owner renamed it with a corruption of the slang word for crazy, *dingue*. 'The crowd would begin to drift in any time after noon,' wrote its barman Jimmie Charters. 'Sad individuals with hangovers, or small and quiet sober groups of earnest men and women discussing art, which seemed to be an inexhaustible subject. The hangovers took pick-me-ups and the others sipped their drinks slowly, but by five o'clock the crowd was in full swing. Excited women, amorous couples, jittering fairies, gay dogs, over-serious young men expounding theories, and a few quiet, observing souls who took it all in and appreciated it.'

It was here that Donald Ogden Stewart, then a popular writer of humour, and more famous at the time than either Hemingway or Scott Fitzgerald, introduced them early in 1925. These days, it's an Italian restaurant, the Auberge de Venise. A glazed case enshrines some Hemingway memorabilia. The bar is all that remains of the original décor, and a brass plate - placed, incongruously, at ankle level - signifies its role in the Hemingway myth.

THE GERMAN OCCUPATION

L ife under the German Occupation of 1940-44 is the second most popular theme for guided tours of Paris, after Ernest Hemingway, but the city has relatively few memorials to those years. Aside from a modest Museum of the Occupation and another devoted to the Holocaust, the most common reminders are discreet marble tablets scattered about the city that signify a resistant died there *pour la Patrie* (for the homeland). Almost all date from August 1944, when citizens of Paris, anticipating the arrival of the Allies, rose against the already retreating Germans. Despite General de Gaulle's passionate speech celebrating 'Paris liberated! Liberated by itself, liberated by its people,' between 1940 and 1944 a mere 2 per cent of the population played any significant part in the Resistance. Most were too busy just getting by. Albert Camus, in his novel *The Fall*, commented bleakly that joining the Resistance seemed like 'being asked to do some weaving in a cellar, for days and nights on end, until some brutes should come to haul me from hiding, undo my weaving and then drag me to another cellar to beat me to death. I admired those who indulged in such heroism of the depths but couldn't imitate them.'

Although post-war films and fiction depict the Resistance as a well-organized clandestine army, it comprised a number of groups, each with its own agenda, and often mutually hostile. Best organized were the communists, who hoped to turn their wartime activities into peacetime power and influence. They were joined by criminals who escaped from prison and joined the *maquis*, named for the undergrowth in which partisans hid. Some went on to criminal careers, including the Corsican Jean Jehan, who would mastermind the heroin smuggling operation dramatized in the 1971 film *The French Connection*.

Germany occupied only the coasts and principal cities, leaving administration of the rest to a puppet government located in the spa city of Vichy, and headed by the First World War hero Marshal Philippe Pétain. Hitler planned, after the war, to make France a cash cow, feeding the Reich, while at the same time maintaining its entertainment, wine and fashion industries, and preserving Paris and the Côte d'Azur as resorts. In the meantime, Germany systematically looted the nation, and deported its young men of military age to work in its factories. In a final indignity, France was forced to pay the costs of maintaining the occupying forces.

Paris's most luxurious accommodations were commandeered. The Luftwaffe chose the Palais du Luxembourg, digging up its formal gardens and planting vegetables. The military governor grabbed the eighteenth-century hotel, Le Meurice, while the Abwehr counter-intelligence service of Admiral Wilhelm Canaris chose the Hôtel Lutetia. Leading collaborators socialized at the Ritz, where Reichsmarschall Hermann Göring occupied the Royal Suite while he selected which masterpieces to send back to Berlin.

With almost all produce shipped to Germany, Parisians struggled to feed themselves. The actress Leslie Caron, then a child, remembered the experience vividly.

We ate animal fodder: salsify, rutabagas, Jerusalem artichoke. Fruit was as rare and expensive as tobacco. Children had one glass of milk a day. We were each given an ever-shrinking ration of butter; it eventually amounted to an eggcup-full per person, per week. By the end of the war, bread was down to one slice a day per person – two-thirds flour, one-third wood shavings. Meat was also extremely scarce: about two hundred grams a week each. Cats and dogs disappeared – they were stolen and eaten. As a pharmacist, my father received cocoa butter to make suppositories, and it became the substitute for butter and oil in our cooking. Everything at our table had a faint cocoa flavour.

The occupiers allowed France's flourishing show business to continue, under supervision. Films continued to be made, including some, in particular Marcel Carné's epic of eighteenth-century theatre and crime, *Les enfants du paradis*, which would be hailed as masterpieces. Having accepted the reality of occupation, celebrities often chose to make the best of it. Couturier Coco Chanel shared her suite at the Ritz with Baron Hans Günther von Dincklage, chosen by Hitler to manage France's textile industry. Arletty and Mireille Balin were among the actresses who took German lovers, with Arletty – another Ritz tenant – excusing her behaviour with a famous quip: 'My heart is French but my ass in international.' Jailed after the war, she would be brought in handcuffs to the studio to re-record dialogue for *Les enfants du paradis*.

Berlin encouraged French writers to continue working, even inviting them to conferences in Germany where they could feel part of a wider but German-dominated literary community. Some collaborated more enthusiastically than others. Pierre Drieu la Rochelle accepted editorship of the important literary monthly *Nouvelle Revue Française* and Robert Brasillach of the pro-Nazi magazine *Je suis partout* (I Am Everywhere). Jean Cocteau, 'openly and comfortably gay', wrote one historian, 'moved in all the best circles. His need for attention and his easy morals got him rides in the limousines of many wealthy Parisians and occupiers who found him amusing.'

Café owners turned cellars into nightclubs for the occupiers. The Luftwaffe officer placed in charge of entertaining the troops, Dietrich Schulz-Köhn, had been a familiar figure in Paris pre-war jazz circles. Faced with the problem that Hitler had declared jazz 'decadent' and, in addition, that the best players were Jewish, Roma or African, all proscribed under Nazi racial laws, he resourcefully designated them *wirtschaftlich wertvolle* (economically valuable), removing the risk of deportation. Grateful musicians named him 'Doctor Jazz'. Django Reinhardt, France's biggest jazz star, and a Roma, was on tour in England when the Germans invaded, and could have sat out the war there. Instead he returned to Paris and played throughout the Occupation.

Among painters, Picasso and Matisse remained in the city, protected by art-loving Nazis. Singers Maurice Chevalier, Tino Rossi, Édith Piaf, Charles Trenet and club owner Suzy Solidor all performed for Nazi audiences and broadcast on German-controlled Radio Paris. 'We understood that terrible things were happening in Poland and Austria,' Chevalier said, 'but Parisians don't really care about anything but Paris. I guess we feel we are doing our share by giving laughter and gaiety to the nation.'

Anglophile writer Bernard Fay, a fanatical Catholic who was later convicted for involvement in the deaths of fifty anti-Catholic freemasons, intervened to save Gertrude Stein and Alice Toklas, relocating them in the remote village of Culoz, under the protection of the local *commissaire de police*. In gratitude, Stein translated some of Marshal Pétain's speeches and suggested to her American editor that he publish them. Fortunately for her reputation, he refused. Unlike many literary and artistic collaborators who were jailed for periods ranging from a few days to some months, then quietly released, Fay remained in prison until 1951, when Alice Toklas secretly funded his escape to Switzerland. The only prominent writer executed for collaboration was Robert Brasillach, shot by firing squad. His last words were *'Vive la France quand même!'* (Long live France anyway).

BEAUTY IN THE STREETS
1968 AND ITS EVENEMENTS

I n the spring of 1968, France came to a halt as the people battled over its future. Students fought teachers, workers fought bosses, filmmakers fought bureaucrats, and the police and militia of the CRS (Compagnies républicaines de sécurité) fought everyone. Universities closed. Trains stopped running, and most newspapers were no longer printed. News of the uprising sparked similar protests around the world. And at the height of the argument, the head of state disappeared.

Then, after six weeks, it ended. What began with every appearance of civil war petered out into something more like a noisy national debate. As one politician remarked in surprise, it was the first revolution in history in which nobody died. In fact, the word 'revolution' was no longer mentioned. Instead, people spoke of '*les evenements*' (the events) of 1968.

'The French believe that all errors are distant, someone else's fault,' wrote American critic Adam Gopnik, but in 1968, although nations all over the world would soon be blaming France for igniting unrest among their own young people, the French had nobody to blame but themselves. Reasons for their dissatisfaction were numerous. Technology had accelerated progress in industry but wages hadn't caught up. Education, preoccupied with formal learning, enshrined the values of another century. Many school leavers of the working class who might have gone to college took dead-end jobs in the post office or the railways. Their disillusion was reflected in such songs as Serge Gainsbourg's 1958 '*Le Poinçonneur des Lilas*' (The Ticket Clipper of Lilas Station). 'Some guys go to Miami./ Meanwhile I do my duty/ At the bottom of the cellar./ Can you imagine a more stupid job?/ I make holes in tickets.'

As the Communist Party increased in influence, the conservative administration of Charles de Gaulle stifled debate. Many felt he cared more for his role as a statesman, intervening in the affairs of French Canada and Algeria but ignoring issues closer to home. Apparently trivial domestic problems became exaggerated. In February, the Minister for Cultural Affairs André Malraux fired Henri Langlois, head of the Cinémathèque Française and ideologue of the *nouvelle vague*. He was reinstated after protests from François Truffaut, Jean-Luc Godard and the other filmmakers he had inspired, but Malraux's high-handedness continued to rankle.

The flashpoint came at the Université Paris-Nanterre, in the left-wing *ceinture rouge* (red belt) ringing Paris. On 8 January, as François Missoffe, Minister of Youth and Sports, opened a new swimming pool, a student, Daniel Cohn-Bendit, demanded to know why male students couldn't visit their girlfriends in the female dormitories. Missoffe ducked the question. Over the following days, other complaints surfaced, of repressive university policies and the admission of police onto the campus to arrest an alleged terrorist. In March, Cohn-Bendit (aka Danny Le Rouge – Danny the Red) – fortuitously, his red hair matched his politics – formed the March 22 Movement and led an occupation of the dormitories.

On 2 May, the dean shut down Paris-Nanterre. The following day, 2,000 students at France's oldest university, the Sorbonne, occupied their building in sympathy. 1,500 police tried to eject them, with illiberal use of their batons or *matraques*. Seventy-two students were wounded, 600

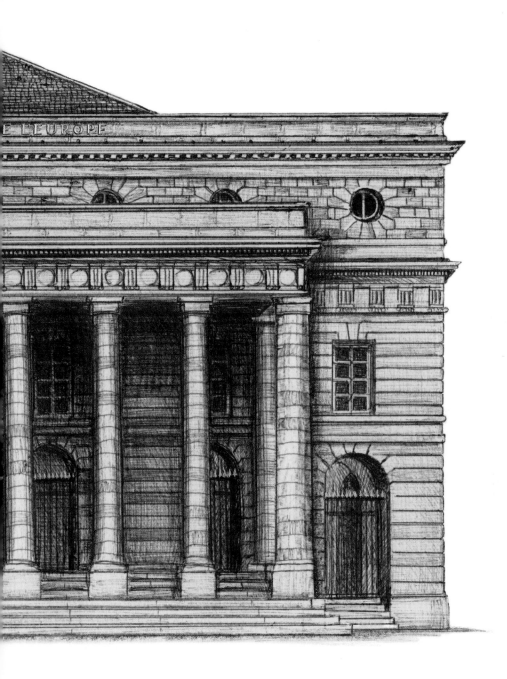

detained for questioning, and thirteen arrested. When the rector decided, three weeks before final exams, to close the Sorbonne also, students surged into the streets, looking for a place to meet. The Theatre de l'Odéon, a branch of the national theatre, the Comédie Française, became their headquarters, initially with the agreement of its manager, veteran theatre and film actor Jean-Louis Barrault. He even gave a speech of welcome, a conciliatory gesture that was to rebound on him.

Within a few days, most of the country was on strike. Without newspapers and only limited broadcast media, citizens relied on gossip and the rhetoric of student ideologues. There was much talk of transforming education. Students criticized the *lycée* system of public schooling, seen as elitist. Some called for 'People's Universities'. Graffiti and posters spread the students' message. A masked CRS man with shield and raised *matraque* appeared on posters all over Paris. The image of a man's shocked, bloodstained face was captioned '*Bourgeois, vous n'avez rien compris*' (Bourgeois, you have understood nothing). Other slogans and posters shrilled '*La société est une fleur carnivore*' (Society is a carnivorous flower), '*Pouvoir à l'imagination*' (All power to the imagination) and '*Il est interdit d'interdire*' (It is forbidden to forbid). The image of a girl caught in the act of flinging a cobblestone bore the message '*La beauté est dans la rue*' (Beauty is in the streets).

Students felled trees along Boulevard Saint-Michel to create barricades from behind which they derided the police and militia. A popular chant suggested that CRS stood for '*connards racistes salopards*' (assholes racists bastards). Street battles on the night of 10 May left 367 injured and over 5,000 under arrest. On 11 May, on rue Gay-Lussac alone, eighty cars were torched. The next day, locals, the day's *baguette* in hand, wandered bemused among the wreckage. The stink of burned automobiles hung over the city. It was anarchy, madness, destruction – and the most excitement Paris had experienced since 1944.

Reports of police brutality prompted the trade unions to strike and occupy factories. At rallies and marches, protestors demanded amnesty for demonstrators, political freedom for trade unions, reform of education and the introduction of an economic system 'by and for the people'. Partly in protest at Henri Langlois' dismissal, but also motivated by its outmoded methods of selection, Jean-Luc Godard and François Truffaut led an attack on the Cannes Film Festival. Physically clinging to the curtains at the opening screening, they prevented any films from being shown.

Inside the Theatre de l'Odéon, chaos reigned. Students ripped up the red velvet upholstery and looted the costume store. Clothing intended for productions of Voltaire and Racine became fancy dress. A Committee of Occupation urged 'the systematic sabotage of the cultural industry, especially the industry of show business, in order to make room for true collective creation. Never again must a ticket be sold in the ex-theatre of France. The only theatre is guerrilla theatre!'

Barrault tried to reason with the student leaders. What exactly was 'guerrilla theatre'? Who would perform it, and where? What of actors and technicians? They were workers too. How were they to earn a living?

'If the Odéon is an "ex-theatre",' he concluded, 'then those who work in it must be "ex-people". But here is a living creature named Barrault in front of you! What are you going to do about us?' Nobody had an answer.

These were not President de Gaulle's finest hours. Demonstrations and civil disobedience offended his sense of order. In an angry speech, he called for 'La réforme oui, la chienlit non' (Reform, yes, misrule, no). *Chienlit* was a medieval carnival during which a fool was placed on the throne for a day as a Lord of Misrule. But split up as '*chie-en-lit*', it could mean 'to shit in the bed'. Neither students nor striking workers liked this comparison, and the phrase would haunt de Gaulle.

On the morning of 29 May, he vacated the Élysée, telling his staff, 'Nobody attacks an empty palace.' For the rest of the day, his whereabouts were unknown. In fact, he had flown by helicopter to Germany to consult General Jacques Massu, commanding the French Army on the Rhine. If martial law was declared, would the army back him? Massu promised its support but de Gaulle never played this card: wisely, since a survey found that only 5 per cent of voters would have supported military intervention. Thirty-three per cent would have opposed it, while the rest of the country would have done nothing.

Instead, he called an election. Tempers cooled among students and workers in expectation of a change in government. Factories reopened. Newspapers and broadcast media came back on line. Students halted street demonstrations. The police retook the Sorbonne on 16 June. With the weather warmer and the result of the election apparently a foregone conclusion, thoughts turned to *les vacances*.

On 23 and 30 June, France went to the polls. The communists, who had decided not to risk a takeover in May, were astonished when de Gaulle scored the most sweeping victory in French parliamentary history, taking

353 of 486 seats, to their meagre thirty-four and the Socialists' fifty-seven. France had voted for a return to normal and the re-establishment of what really mattered to its people – their quality of life.

In time, the events of 1968 did change France. De Gaulle retired. Industry produced more, although that was inevitable as the European Union gained momentum. Education became more liberal. Additional television channels appeared. The Cannes Film Festival changed its policies to admit work by new directors. Less ostentatiously, the city decided enough cobbles had been thrown at its peace officers and began to cover 680ha of paved streets with bitumen.

As André Malraux fired him as director of the Odéon, citing his speech of welcome to the invading students, Jean-Louis Barrault realized he and the theatre had been pawns in a political game. By throwing the Odéon to the students 'like a bone to a dog', Malraux gambled they would spare more prestigious locations such as the presidential palace. Refusing to be cowed, Barrault relocated in the derelict Gare d'Orsay and launched an innovative programme that restored his reputation. Daniel Cohn-Bendit would enter politics and become a member of the European Parliament. And everyone else went to the seaside.

DIANA, DODI, DAVID AND THE DUCHESS
BRITS AND ROYALS IN PARIS

In August 1997, Diana, Britain's former Princess of Wales, and her lover Dodi Fayed flew into Paris from St Tropez. The next day, they visited a mansion on the edge of the Bois de Boulogne, once the home of the Duke of Windsor, who, as Edward VIII, abdicated in 1936 and went into exile rather than give up his American mistress. Dodi's father, Mohamed Al-Fayed, an admirer of the British royal family, owned the house and commissioned its restoration, but Dodi and Diana didn't stay long, preferring a suite at the Ritz, another possession of Al-Fayed *père*. Leaving the hotel that night, pursued by paparazzi, the chauffeur crashed their Mercedes in a tunnel below the Pont de l'Alma. Diana, Dodi and the chauffeur, Henri Paul, died.

By chance, the accident took place under a riverside plaza where, in 1989, the city, to celebrate Franco-American friendship, installed a model of the Statue of Liberty's torch. The monument looked like becoming a white elephant but Diana's death gave it new purpose. The plaza was renamed Square Princess Diana, and the torch, its American connection forgotten, became a reminder of a British life passed, as Elton John sang at her memorial service, 'like a candle in the wind'.

The visit of Diana and Dodi to a house where another member of the royal family once lived in exile was a reminder that British aristocracy often took refuge in Paris. Waiting to ascend the throne, Queen Victoria's son spent so much time in its brothels that comedians, with memories of

his pious precursor, Edward the Confessor, christened him 'Edward the Caresser'. Half a century later, the former Edward VIII – who was called David (one of his given names) by his family and friends – also made his home there, bribed to stay away with a generous allowance and the title Duke of Windsor. But like his duchess, who wore clothes by Elsa Schiaparelli, Christian Dior and Paco Rabanne but otherwise remained remote from the French, the duke scorned his hosts. When invasion forced him even further into exile, first to Spain and then to the Bahamas as Governor General (a posting the duchess compared to Napoleon's imprisonment on St Helena), he told a friend that France capitulated because it was 'internally diseased'.

After the war, the Windsors resumed life in Paris. In 1952, they moved into the estate where Charles de Gaulle lived after liberation. It became their home for the rest of their leisured lives, except for weekends and holidays spent at a converted mill at Gif-sur-Yvette, next door to former British fascist leader Oswald Mosley and his aristocratic wife Diana Mitford, and their summer retreat at Château de la Croë on Cap d'Antibes.

Depending on the time of year, between 200,000 and 400,000 British people live in France, about 20,000 of them in Paris. The rich have visited for centuries. They bought houses from which to embark on the Grand Tour, raced horses, collected art, and relaxed in its restaurants and brothels. Unlike Britain, France condoned prostitution, homosexuality and inter-racial relationships, and placed no restriction on drug use. Nor did it forbid the publication and sale of pornography – providing it was written in a language other than French.

The author Ford Madox Ford grumbled about the 'Haussmannised' city but enjoyed its casual immorality, which he shared, briefly, in a *ménage à trois* with fellow novelist Jean Rhys and his Australian mistress Stella Bowen. He was typical of the leisured and gifted who looked to Paris for sensual refreshment. Others included Sir Arthur Sullivan, of the team of Gilbert and Sullivan, and Oscar Wilde, the greatest wit of the day.

Many expatriates gravitated to the Mediterranean Riviera, 'a sunny place for shady people' in the words of novelist William Somerset Maugham, who, along with Aldous Huxley, E. Phillips Oppenheim, Frank Harris, Edith Wharton and scores of other British and American intellectuals, joined the addicts, erotomanes, refugees, terrorists and criminals basking in the French tradition of *laissez-faire*. American humourist James Thurber, a journalist on the Riviera in 1925/6, wrote nostalgically that 'Nice, in that indolent winter, was full of knaves and rascals, adventurers and imposters, *pochards* and *indiscrets*, whose ingenious exploits, sometimes in full masquerade costume, sometimes in the nude, were easy and pleasant to report.' Generally, the police ignored all but the most flagrant crimes, but should they take notice, the African coast and freedom was a short sea voyage away.

In novels and films, most Americans who come to France, from John Gilbert in *The Big Parade* (1925) and Gene Kelly in *An American in Paris* (1951) to Lily Collins in *Emily in Paris* (2020), adjust well, and find love with a local. Britons are conspicuously less successful, committing *gaffes* which Americans just shrug off. Archetypal Brit Alec Guinness suffered repeatedly on his cinematic visits. In *The Scapegoat* (1959), he encounters his doppelganger, a shady aristo, and adopts his persona, problems and mistress. As *Father Brown – Detective* (1954), he unmasks another crooked count as an international art thief. His middle-aged *roué* in *To Paris, with Love* (1955) takes his son across the Channel to find him a girlfriend but instead acquires one himself, while, as an amateur bank robber in *The Lavender Hill Mob* (1951), he's caught because he doesn't know that the French and English pronounce the letter 'r' differently. Alfred Hitchcock's *The Lady Vanishes* (1938) has perhaps the classic depiction of the English abroad in fanatical cricket fans Basil Radford and Naunton Wayne, trampling foreign sensibilities ('Third rate country. No wonder they have revolutions') in pursuit of the latest test match score.

Given this catalogue of *contretemps*, it seems appropriate that Diana, that embodiment of British beauty, charm and irresponsibility, should find death rather than love in Paris, but also a kind of immortality, and that the place of her passing, a tunnel by the Seine, should be marked by an unearned eternal flame.

IN THE SHADOWS

OPIUM

Asia fascinated the European art establishment throughout the late nineteenth and early twentieth centuries. Claude Monet and Henri de Toulouse-Lautrec admired Japanese woodcut prints, first seen in Europe as wrapping paper for imported porcelain. Such writers as Pierre Loti, Pierre Louÿs and Claude Farrère created a vision of China and Japan as cultures of sage philosophers and sexually accomplished courtesans. France's provinces of Cochinchina, Annam and Tonkin, in what is now Vietnam and Cambodia, provided painters, writers and composers with a rich source of inspiration. But it was the poetry of Charles Baudelaire that brought these together by celebrating the 'artificial paradises' to be found in the smoke from an opium pipe.

When Thomas de Quincey published his 1821 *Confessions of an English Opium Eater*, the drug was already widely known and abused by European artists. Alfred de Musset smoked it. Lord Byron drank laudanum, a solution of 10 per cent opium dissolved in spiced alcohol. Indo-Chinese Yunnan opium was much preferred to the cruder Benares variety – 'English Mud' – of which the British East India Company enjoyed a monopoly. Successive rulers in China stamped out opium use but, in the Opium Wars of the 1840s, the company forced them to lift import duties on the drug, which it then traded for China's most precious export, tea.

Chinese workers on the goldfields and railroads brought opium to the United States and the countries of the British Empire. *Fumeries* (smoking houses) were soon a feature of every port city. In London, urbane drug lord 'Brilliant' Chang controlled an empire that stretched from the docklands district of Limehouse to fashionable Regent Street, where he owned one of the city's first Chinese restaurants. Sydney, Australia, had twenty-five *fumeries*, while most pharmacies sold laudanum, which became the preferred remedy of the highly-strung, the Prozac of its day. Although opium's chemically refined forms of morphine and heroin provided a faster, more intense sensation, artists and thinkers preferred the drug raw. It allowed them to drift for hours in a world transmuted into pure movement and form. Nearer our time, mescaline, peyote and LSD had the same appeal to intellectuals and aesthetes, with a similar promise of transcendence.

To a culture that created the vine-like curlicues of Art Nouveau, Monet's water lilies and Debussy's evocation in music of fountains, clouds and the sea, it was the ideal narcotic – organic, transcendent and ostensibly benign. Jean Cocteau, who smoked as many as sixty pipes a day, celebrated the drug's capacity to make time stand still. The nineteenth century introduced man to only one entirely new sensation – speed. Opium was its necessary antithesis. 'Everything one does in life,' he wrote, 'even love, occurs in an express train racing toward death. To smoke opium is to escape from the train while it is still moving. It is to concern oneself with something other than life or death.'

Since one of the first and most powerful effects of opium is physical weakness, *fumeries* provided cots or mats on which to recline, and staff to refill pipes and rehydrate clients with tea. In Paris, the most fashionable was Drosso's, in a secluded location near the Bois de Boulogne, a favourite of writer/publisher Harry Crosby. His wife Caresse described it as 'a series of small fantastic rooms, large satin divans heaped with pillows, walls covered with gold-embroidered arras, in the centre of each room a low round stand on which was ranged all the paraphernalia of the pipe ... The air was sweet with the smell of opium.' After they'd changed into kimonos, Harry sprawled on a couch with one arm around a pretty French girl. Caresse snuggled under the other. With each pipe, the real world receded a little more. 'Smiling, one relaxed and drowsed,' Caresse wrote, 'another's arms about one, it mattered little whose.'

Home opium parties were popular with the *jeunesse dorée* (wealthy and fashionable young people) in the period after the First World War. To lounge near-naked in your home and surrender to your most corrupt desires transgressed every rule of polite society, a prospect the young, rich and entitled embraced with appetite. When 'Brilliant' Chang supplied opium for a party, it came with a hostess, generally young, attractive and white, to demonstrate the correct way to smoke it. In his novel *Dope*, Sax Rohmer described such a tutorial.

Mrs Sin carefully lighted the lamp, which burned with a short, bluish flame, and, opening the lacquered box, she dipped the spatula into the thick gummy substance which it contained and twisted the little instrument round and round between her fingers, presently withdrawing it with a globule about the size of a bean adhering to the end.

She began to twirl the prepared opium above the flame. From it a slight, sickly smelling vapor arose. When by evaporation the drug had become reduced to the size of a small pea, and a vague spirituous blue flame began to dance round the end of the spatula, Mrs. Sin pressed it adroitly into the tiny bowl of one of the ivory pipes, having first held the bowl inverted for a moment over the lamp.

She turned to Rita. 'The guest of the evening,' she said. 'Do not be afraid. Inhale – oh, so gentle – and blow the smoke from the nostrils.'

In the late 1920s, when Hungarian photographer Gyula Halasz (aka Brassaï) created *Paris de Nuit*, his classic documentation of the city's *demi-monde*, his exploration took him to a *fumerie*. Among its clients was an actress. Brassaï asked to take her picture. Her response condenses the sense of opium smokers as privileged, set apart.

Of course! And you have my permission to print it. I'm proud to smoke ... They say that after a while drugs, opium, will destroy you, make you thin, weaken you, ruin your mind, your memory; that it makes you stagger, gives you a yellow complexion, sunken eyes, all of that... Rot! Look at me. And tell me frankly, am I not beautiful and desirable? Well, let me tell you, I've smoked opium for ten years, and I'm doing all right.

SPENDING A PENNY

THE PISSOIR AND DAMES PIPIS

'Here I sit, broken-hearted/ Paid a penny – only farted.' This poignant couplet, once a popular toilet graffito, recalls the days when 'spending a penny' was a euphemism for visiting the lavatory. That one should expect to pay for relief went without saying. British industrial wisdom succinctly articulates 'Where there's muck, there's brass,' a truth grasped as early as the first century by Emperor Titus Flavius Vespasianus. Noting that tanners paid nothing for the urine they harvested from Rome's public urinals to use in preparing leather, he imposed a tax. In his honour, the French called urinals *vespasiennes*.

Paris lagged in the provision of public lavatories. Defecation wasn't regarded as something that necessarily required privacy. In 1589, a monk fatally knifed King Henri III when he invited him in for an audience while seated on his commode. The nineteenth-century city provided 'barrels of easement' for men who needed to urinate but those wishing to defecate were advised, counter-intuitively, to do so *facing* a wall – so that nobody would see their faces. For anyone desiring privacy, entrepreneurs with mobile toilets stationed themselves at intersections. The travelling commode, a variation on the sedan chair, offered relief in comfort, with a retractable seat and a chamber pot. Women were less fortunate. As crinolines made them too bulky to squeeze inside, they had to make do with squatting under a tent-like canvas cloak that draped them from neck to ground.

Individual public urinals appeared in 1843. A hollow column, open on one side, with a simple ground-level drain, they were built of stone and ornately decorated. Georges-Eugène Haussmann, charged by Emperor Napoleon III (great-nephew of Napoleon Bonaparte) with modernizing the city, replaced them with the *pissoir*. All-steel, and consisting of a trough behind a knee-to-neck screen, they were easy to clean and could accommodate more than one person at a time. Being so public discouraged their use as homosexual meeting points, the practice known in Britain as 'cottaging', but in such areas as Pigalle, street prostitutes loitered nearby, making eye contact with potential clients over the screen.

Author Henry Miller was an enthusiastic patron of prostitutes and *pissoirs* both. 'Standing behind a tin strip,' he wrote, 'and looking out on the throng with that contented, easy, vacant smile, that long reminiscent pleasurable look, is a good thing ... Standing thus with heart and fly and bladder open, I seem to recall every urinal I ever stepped into. To relieve a full bladder is one of the great human joys.' He particularly patronized a facility near the Jardin du Luxembourg, from which he could spy on Parisians enjoying the sun.

In the 1930s, Paris had 1,230 *pissoirs*, a number that, by 1966, had dwindled to 329. Today, only one survives. This lonely throwback stands outside the grim walls of the Santé prison. The automated toilets, technically

known as Sanisettes, that replaced them were a mixed blessing. These unisex cabins, originally coin-operated but now free, function with a ponderous efficiency that seldom accords with the urgent needs of their clients. Every week, a few newbies, jumping the cycle by ducking through an open door as the last user departs, discover, to their dismay, that they not only flush after each use but also deluge the walls, floor – and occupant, if any – with a high-pressure spray.

Pissoirs didn't accommodate women, but from the early twentieth century a few facilities in the city's wealthier districts offered female relief – at a price. The Lavatory de la Madeleine, under Place de la Madeleine, embodied luxury. Built in 1904 by Porcher and Company, who proudly signed their work in Art Nouveau lettering embedded in the wall, it has been restored and is once again open for business. It boasts varnished mahogany woodwork, stained-glass windows, ornate ceramics, mosaics, brass fittings, floor-to-ceiling tiles and a shoeshine stand. A female attendant is also in residence, comfortably installed in a windowed office – a contrast to the *dames pipis* of cafés and hotels, stern guardians who once grudgingly provided a scrap of towel and fragment of soap before pointedly presenting their saucer for a tip. '*Dame pipi* evokes a pejorative image,' says Lavatory de la Madeleine's modern proprietor. 'I'm old enough to remember the lady sitting in her stall, waiting for change, barely saying hello or goodbye. Our staff welcomes the customer, orients them and cleans the toilets after every use. It's not the same job at all.'

In 2015, when only four staffed public toilets survived in Paris and the city outsourced their cleaning to a Dutch company, the last surviving *dames pipis* went on strike. It was an empty gesture. Visitors had learned to use café toilets, paying the traditional price of a quick *café express* at the bar. Most such facilities are unisex, but for those alarmed at having to share with a hairy biker or a stiff-necked matron, there are always the deluxe accommodations of the Madeleine.

Recently, the newest installed Sanisettes have acquired a refinement. Tacked on to the existing mechanised cabinet is an old fashioned *pissoir*. In this as in so much more, it seems Haussmann was right all along.

THE SECRET CITIZENS

They're everywhere. By the hundreds of thousands. Millions even. On the Eiffel Tower, inside the Louvre, under the colonnades of the Palais Royal. One can't go anywhere without bumping into them. Even inside medieval churches, crawling in and out of the ancient stone work, gnawing at the sacred symbols of Christianity ...

Rats!

Improbable though it may sound, Paris is the fourth most rat-infested city in the world, after Deshnoke in India, London and New York. It has more rats than people; an estimated six million, about two for each inhabitant. One gloomy statistician speculated that, in the city's most populous corners, an example of *Rattus rattus* is never more than a metre away.

The French share the common condemnation of rats, but can't help finding them interesting, sometimes morbidly so. Marcel Proust, whose epicurean elegance disguised an often sinister interest in the perverse, derived sexual satisfaction from watching husky young men torture caged rats with red-hot hatpins, a fact that Jean Cocteau gleefully put about after having encountered him in one of the fetish hotels Proust part-owned.

The term 'rat' crops up in the strangest places. Albert Camus used an infestation of rats in his novel *The Plague* as a metaphor for the German Occupation. 'Rats' was how the ballet world designated the painfully thin pre-teen ballerinas-in-waiting who so fascinated Edgar Degas. A rat is also the fibrous pad which, as part of a hairdo, allowed women to wind their hair into the 1970s *bouffant* or beehive, integral to the sack dress or *chemise* fashion, pioneered by Balenciaga, that helped Brigitte Bardot win her international following.

That rats are also edible – their meat is said to taste something like duck – making them even more interesting to the French. In times of sailing ships, naval officers fattened them for eating, feeding them on crumbs from the hard bread known as ship's biscuit, as well the weevils and other insects that made their home in it. In 1871, when the Prussians laid siege to Paris, citizens ate them. Amateur butchers set up stalls in the street, offering to joint a rodent to order.

The 2007 film *Ratatouille* brought rats back to the headlines. Only in Paris would a rat with gourmet cooking skills find appreciation, even respect.

Not only that, but he calls on its rodent community to help, leading to scenes of rat-infested kitchens that would have food inspectors on the verge of collapse. Animator and director Brad Bird, boldly, doesn't glamourize his rats. They are hairy, squat and pink-nosed, with prominent front teeth – and, puzzlingly, New York Lower East side accents.

One of the oddest manifestation of rats is as *boules aux rats* or rat balls. These decorative carvings, apparently unique to France, appear infrequently in churches of the fifteenth and sixteenth centuries. Generally they show groups of rats creeping in and out of – or, sometimes, gnawing on – religious images, notably the Cross. Only nine are known, but others may not have survived their encounter with a hammer and chisel. The most accessible in Paris is in the church of Saint-Germain l'Auxerrois, next to the Louvre, traditionally the church of the Three Musketeers. Access to the inner courtyard is limited, and only by appointment, but those admitted are shown, high up on the north side of the courtyard, a water spout in the form of a gargoyle. It sticks out from the wall at a right angle, with a

gaping mouth from which water erupts during a rain storm. The supporting buttress is carved in the form of a sphere, surmounted by a cross, around and through which rats swarm, watched by an alert cat.

Sacrilegious carvings, often erotic or scatological, occasionally appear in medieval buildings; private jokes by bored or malicious sculptors, never meant to be seen. But rat balls are always in plain sight. Another, in the southern city of Carpentras, sits above what's known as the Jewish Door of the Cathédrale St-Siffrein, through which Jews who had converted to Christianity were permitted to enter and hear Mass. That carving is assumed to be antisemitic but a former Paris priest of Saint-Germain l'Auxerrois has a more charitable explanation for the Parisian example. It could mean, he suggests, 'that, even though it was saved by the cross of Christ, the world is still the prey of evil, personified by five big rats with their long hairy tails. The rats which gnaw the ball from the inside – symbolizing sin – get out of it from the holes they made. A cat, referring to the Devil, lies above the ball and watches over its prey, waiting for the right moment to pounce on them.'

It's not stone rats, however, that pose Paris's worst vermin problem. Particularly since the Covid pandemic, the living variety have become increasingly audacious, in particular attacking the plastic bags of public refuse holders in search of food scraps. Signs urge people to ditch their edible refuse out of rat reach, but with little effect.

Some theories of their proliferation blame the European Union's crackdown on the pesticides that formerly limited the rodent population; others the city's policy of preserving ancient buildings, since it also conserves the nooks and crannies where rats breed. It's also likely that a rise in water levels has driven them from their subterranean lairs. The numbers that swarm around riverbank sites, including the Square du Vert-Galant, at the foot of the Île de la Cité, support this. Dark as death, the Seine sucks at the ancient stones edging this tiny park. A willow trails fronds in the water that the breeze disturbs, obscuring and revealing like a curtain the lights of the Louvre on the opposite bank. Lit by street lamps on Pont Neuf and the headlights of passing cars, rats scuttle by the water line, indifferent to both history and art. When all this has sunk back to the ooze, they will survive.

THE LEFT HAND OF TOURISM
CRIME IN POST-WAR PARIS

Crime was a growth industry in post-First World War Paris. The term 'lost generation', which Gertrude Stein applied to the expatriate writers of Paris in the 1920s, had originally referred to the young French men and women who, deprived of an education by the war and with no job prospects in a weakened economy, drifted into prostitution, gambling and theft.

Sniffing rich pickings in the influx of foreigners after the First World War, villains gravitated to Montparnasse. As early as 1914, Guillaume Apollinaire lamented that 'all the hashish-eaters, opium smokers and the inevitable sniffers of ether, plus anyone else who's been expelled from a Montmartre being destroyed by landlords and architects, have moved, along with people of the same kind, wherever they come from'.

Professional criminals ranged from the Bonnot Gang – anarchists for whom robbing banks was an act of economic sabotage – through burglars and assassins, to pickpockets, bag-snatchers and pimps who, excluded from reputable *maisons closes* (closed houses), lurked in hotels and bars, ready to arrange a pornographic movie show or sexual exhibition, or deliver a *poule de luxe* (high-class prostitute) to your room.

Art had a school of crime all to itself. Entire workshops of forgers turned out phoney Renoirs and Van Goghs. Camille Corot, in particular, was extensively faked. In 1926, a cache of 2,400 spurious Corot drawings came to light, all from the hand of the same productive counterfeiter. Cynics joked that, of Corot's 3,000 known works, 5,000 were in the United States.

In a popular swindle, a prospective buyer, visiting the studio of a supposedly brilliant young artist, found him working with an attractive nude model. While the painter blustered about being disturbed, the model took her time slipping into her *peignoir* (negligee), leaving the client so confused that he bought the worthless canvas, leaving the artist to prop another painting on the easel and wait with his mistress for their friend, the guide, to arrive with another victim.

Visitors from authoritarian societies, notably Russia, found the spectacle of lawlessness far more piquant than sex. For them, guides provided what became known as the Tour of the Grand Dukes. Should an execution be scheduled at the Santé prison, a select few, for an exorbitant

fee, could climb to an attic overlooking the prison yard and watch, often next to a weeping wife or *petite amie* (girlfriend), as the condemned was led to the guillotine.

Sisley Huddleston, long-time Paris correspondent of the London *Times*, described how, if no decapitations were scheduled, 'the Russians were conducted to faked apache [street gang] dens. There were the red-aproned golden-casqued girls, and the sinister-looking apaches with caps drawn over their eyes. In the course of the dancing, a quarrel would break out. A duel with knives would be fought. The grand dukes had their money's worth of thrills; and then the girls took off their aprons and the men donned respectable hats and went quietly home to bed.'

For tourists from the USA, where violence was commonplace, conmen offered the pornography of history: lost treasures, disinherited marquises and haunted chateaux. As the catacombs were not yet open to the public, a guide led them to a remote corner of the city, down narrow stone stairs and through dripping tunnels to a door with the painted sign 'Catacombs. Private Property' and a faded coat of arms hinting at aristocracy. Inside, in a cellar lined with skeletons, a distinguished gentleman accepted a fee (dollars preferred) to show them around. When a sceptic touched the fresh-looking bones and found they were wax, the 'Duc' loftily informed him the originals had naturally long since crumbled into dust.

Anyone with a lingering thirst for the macabre could visit the Grand Guignol, a tiny theatre on the edge of Montmartre. The brainchild of Oscar Méténier, a former public prosecutor turned pulp writer, it presented plays depicting murder, torture and violent death. So effectively were they staged that *grand guignol* passed into the language as a synonym for any scene of bloody horror. Leading lady Paula Maxa, 'the world's most assassinated woman', estimated that over twenty years she was murdered more than 10,000 times in at least sixty different ways. From private boxes, often with female company, sexual sadists watched as women were tortured, eyes gouged out, hands and fingers severed, faces burned with acid or pressed to red-hot stoves.

Only a few blocks away, 'ghost show cabarets' with fanciful names – 'The End of the World', 'The Dead Rat', 'The White Wolf', 'The Mad Cow', 'The Cabaret of Nothingness' – also did good business. At the entrance to the 'Cabaret du Néant', a sepulchral voice intoned, 'Welcome, O weary wanderer, to the realm of death! Enter, choose your coffin, and be seated beside it.' In its main bar or *Salle d'intoxication*, tables were shaped like coffins, the chandeliers were of human bones and the waiters wore undertakers' outfits. After a stiff drink, punters were herded into a narrow crypt, the Room of Disintegration, for a demonstration of the stage illusion known as 'Pepper's Ghost', in which, thanks to an angled sheet of glass, a volunteer became a skeleton before their eyes.

Behind these shabby fantasies, true crime was invading the highest levels of government. With a combination of charm, bravado and bribery, the swindler Serge Stavisky sold millions in worthless bonds, backed by the supposed fortunes held in the nation-wide chain of *monts de piété* (municipal pawnshops). A familiar figure around the nightclubs of Montparnasse with his fashion-model wife, Arlette, and his personal bodyguard, Jo Jo 'Le Terreur', Stavisky seemed to live a charmed life, always one step ahead of the police – many of whom were on his payroll. In 1933, after revelations about the extent of the swindle brought down the government, he fled to Switzerland. In January 1934 he was found dead of a gunshot wound in the skiing resort of Chamonix, whether by suicide or killed by the police in a cover-up was never established.

THE DARK FACE OF THE CITY OF LIGHT
SOME MURDERERS

The French take a complacent attitude towards bad behaviour, particularly if it's done with discretion. Most believe that a good marriage will accommodate a few infidelities, that any public official should be free to accept some modest graft, and if the politeness of a servant disguises a secret contempt for his employer ... well, as the saying goes, no man is a hero to his valet, and only a fool should expect otherwise.

It's when people behave against type that the public takes notice. As Robert Browning wrote, 'Our interest's on the dangerous edge of things. The honest thief, the tender murderer, the superstitious atheist.' Nobody cares if a burglar is caught burgling. Nor do the presses stop if a cuckolded husband sticks a knife into his wife, her lover, or even both. But if the burglar gives his spoils to the poor, or the husband joins the guilty lovers in bed, people get interested – as happened with two sensational French murder cases, both in 1933. In February, two sisters, Christine and Léa Papin, murdered their employer and her daughter in a particularly grisly manner, and in August of that year Violette Nozière, a teenager with a stylish taste in clothes, poisoned her parents in Paris's 12th arrondissement. Her mother survived but her father, a railway engine driver, died.

The Papins worked as housemaids in the regional town of Le Mans, employed by René Lancelin, a retired solicitor, his wife Léonie, and their daughter Geneviève. Léonie Lancelin suffered from depression, which made her hypercritical of the women, sometimes assaulting them physically. The sisters, who shared an incestuous sexual relationship, fantasized about wreaking revenge, often sadistic, on their employers, and finally gave in to the impulse after mother and daughter started to punish the weaker Christine. Striking back with scissors, she blinded the daughter. Léa attacked Madame Lancelin, blinding her also. Then the sisters used various weapons, including a knife and a hammer, to finish the job and mutilate their bodies, after which they neatly cleaned up and went to bed, making no attempt to escape.

Violette was a different proposition. With her sullen pout, saucy beret and fur-collared coat, she seemed to embody a generation with no respect for family values. The court heard that she pretended to be rich in order to hang out with the *jeunesse dorée* (wealthy and fashionable young people), and had many affairs, including one with a Black jazz musician. To support her lifestyle, she moonlighted as a prostitute. She persuaded her parents to take a medication that was actually a sedative, and when this didn't kill them, she fed them rat poison.

The trials excited enormous interest. For servants to murder their employers and a child to kill her father struck at the very heart of French society. The press was particularly incensed by Violette, who showed no signs of contrition. 'Everything comes together here,' ranted a magazine, 'the complete absence of morality, the exaggerated taste for profit and pleasure, the unconsciousness of evil, the most atrocious cruelty, the most absolute indifference, devoid of any remorse.'

Public opinion changed after Violette claimed her father had begun sexually abusing her when she was thirteen, infecting her with syphilis. Champions of the working class protested this slur, which was never proved, but intellectuals, the surrealists in particular, took her side. André Breton, who called her 'a flower of the catacombs', published a collection of drawings and texts by, among others, René Magritte and Salvador Dalí, that depicted her as a victim of hypocrisy. None of the group were family men and none had children. Moreover, their emotional lives were often as complicated as those of Violette. Paul Éluard wrote darkly of 'the awful knot of snakes that is blood ties'.

Neither case ended with the expected verdict. As other murders caught the public interest, Violette and the Papins, no longer news, were forgotten. Violette was sentenced to death but was eventually released in 1945 after serving only twelve years. By then, her claim to have been infected with syphilis was decisively disproved, and she went on to have five healthy children.

Despite repeated appeals to be imprisoned in the same jail, the Papin sisters were separated. Christine slipped into depression and died in 1937 of self-starvation. Léa served only eight years, after which she changed her name, took a job as a hotel maid, and lived and died in obscurity. In 1947, interest in the case revived when Jean Genet dramatized their story in *Les Bonnes* (The Maids), the form in which it's best remembered.

Serial murder is uncommon in France. People live too close together; families keep in touch; disappearances are noticed. The country also lacks a transient community of drifters, runaways and street people among whom killers can hide, and who often furnish their prey. The situation is reversed, however, at times of social unrest – which may explain why France's two most notorious mass murderers operated during wartime.

The crimes of Marcel André Henri Félix Petiot are so numerous that one could imagine a jury at his trial announcing, 'We find the defendant *incredibly* guilty.' His crimes, including rape and murder, began in his schooldays. In 1940, despite having only eight months of medical training, he opened a surgery in Paris's staid and fashionable 16th arrondissement, and soon established a trade in fake medical certificates and spurious prescriptions for narcotics.

Once the Germans occupied Paris, he saw an opportunity for even greater profit in the fugitives desperate to get out of France. He had accomplices put it around that a 'Dr Eugene' could arrange visas for South America at 25,000 francs per person. When victims, mostly Jews but also criminals and members of the Resistance, arrived at his surgery, ready to travel, Petiot explained that Argentina demanded a certificate of inoculation, and injected them with cyanide. Police discovered twenty-three corpses in the basement of his Paris home but he's believed to have killed as many as 200.

At first, he dumped their bodies in the Seine. Others were burned or buried in quicklime in his cellar. To friends and relatives of his victims,

Petiot explained that he'd asked them not to communicate with anyone in France for fear of exposing his operation. In a morbidly absurd turn of events, this fooled even the Gestapo, who learned about 'Dr Eugene' but assumed he really was smuggling people and left him at liberty, hoping in time to roll up his entire network. They did arrest three accomplices, but when, under torture, they confessed that people were being murdered rather than smuggled out, the Nazis didn't believe them.

In March 1944, the smell of burning flesh at his home alerted the police, and Petiot's secret was revealed. But 'Dr Eugene' had already disappeared into the chaos of Paris on the eve of D-Day. Under an alias, he approached the disorganized Resistance, which believed his story of having helped numerous fugitives to escape. He was placed in charge of interrogating collaborators now coming forward as the Nazis began pulling out.

Even when the police caught up with him, Petiot maintained the fiction of his 'underground railway'. While insisting that most of his clients were enjoying life in Buenos Aires, he admitted to killing sixty-three people whom he'd unmasked as collaborators or double agents and taken it upon himself to execute. Despite this and other attempts to depict him as a patriot, he was convicted of twenty-six murders, and executed in May 1946. An element of the ridiculous continued to dog Petiot. After each execution, it was the duty of the official executioner to take the guillotine apart and place it in storage. In Petiot's case there were problems putting it back together, and his decapitation was delayed some days until they fixed it.

Absurdity also accompanied the bringing to justice of a second multiple murderer, Henri Désiré Landru. In 1915, as the Great War deteriorated into stalemate, women from all over France volunteered to become *marraines de guerre* (godmothers of war). Choosing a *filleul* (godson) from among troops stationed nearby, they wrote letters, sent small gifts and invited them to visit while on leave. Frequently, these relationship blossomed into something more intimate. One soldier accumulated so many *marraines* that he could only keep them satisfied by deserting.

It used to be thought that the *marraines* movement was a spontaneous gesture by women reaching out to their lonely, homesick defenders. Others suspected a government initiative to placate disgruntled *poilus* (an infantryman). Neither was true. The entire scheme, purely commercial, was the brain-child of Agence Iris, one of France's longest-established matrimonial agencies. It charged *marraines* and *filleuls* for the advertisements they posted, and rented them boxes to hold replies. Business boomed.

Iris never enquired too deeply into its clientele, which had always included prostitutes, abortionists and sellers of fake cures for baldness or impotence. A box at its office also simplified the clandestine correspondence of adulterers. Regular clients included Henry Désiré Landru, a dapper gentleman, well dressed, with a gleaming bald head and mahogany beard. He always placed the same advertisement: 'Widower with two children, aged 43, with comfortable income, serious and moving in good society, desires to meet widow with a view to matrimony.' Nobody enquired why he needed three boxes to handle the replies. In fact, he inserted the same advertisement under ninety different names and responded to approaches from 283 women, ten of whom were never seen again.

Overstretched in wartime, the police gave a low profile to missing persons, particularly as single women often moved without notice. Once Landru's activities were uncovered, his detailed records showed that he personally vetted each candidate. Many he discarded. Some he seduced. Others he murdered; how many will never be known.

His systematic approach was impressive, not to mention his stamina. A typical schedule for 19 May 1915 read:

9.30. Cigarette kiosk Gare de Lyon. Mlle Lydie.
10.30. Café Place St Georges, Mme Ho.----
11.30. Métro Laundry. Mme. Le C-----
14.30. Concorde North-South. Mme Le -----
15.30. Tour St Jacques. Mme Du----
17.30. Mme Va.----
20.15. Saint Lazare. Mme Le ----

Just as tireless in the bedroom, Landru passed his evenings with a succession of these women in one of the seven city and four suburban apartments he maintained in Paris under aliases. Some conquests were simply romantic, but his ten victims had money and, as was customary at a time when only men could have a bank account, signed it over to him as a *dot*, or dowry. Once they accepted his proposal, he suggested they spend a weekend with him in his country house, where he killed and dismembered them, dissolving their bodies in acid or cremating them in the kitchen stove.

Convicting Landru proved difficult. No organic evidence of his victims was ever found; only those metal and glass clips and buttons which acid didn't affect. Imperturbable and elegantly dressed - Louis Aragon suggested, tongue-in-cheek, that his tailor ought to advertise 'M. Landru, when on trial in Paris, is dressed by ...' – Landru mocked the proceedings, and in particular the *juge d'instruction* whose role combined that of trial judge and prosecutor. Visiting him in his chambers, Landru commented on his collection of small Rodin bronzes, then demolished the man by explaining, correctly, that they were fakes.

In the end, simple thrift led to his downfall. He always kept a careful record of expenses, and police noticed that, in taking his victims to the country, he bought return rail tickets for himself but only singles for them. He was executed on 25 February 1922, and this time the guillotine worked perfectly.

PURVEYORS OF PLEASURE

THE GIRL IN THE CHAMPAGNE BATH

It didn't take long for Paris to discover the appetites of the foreign tourists who flooded into the city between the wars. Among these, curiosity about the sex trade figured prominently. *Paris With the Lid Lifted*, a 1929 guide book, recommended visiting a brothel. 'The ladies see no harm in you coming merely to inspect them,' wrote author Bruce Reynolds. 'They will parade for you in frankest nudity, and dance with one another in a mirror-walled room, so that of their charms, you may miss nothing.'

Reynolds also urged women to explore Paris's sexual possibilities. At *thés dansants* (tea dances) in certain hotels, every table had a telephone. Ladies ordered tea, made a choice among the young men seated around the ballroom, summoned one with a phone call and, during a turn on the floor, negotiated the cost of an afternoon upstairs, or perhaps an entire week. 'The gigolo performs his important function in Paris,' Reynolds wrote reassuringly, 'to keep lovely ladies from being lonely and bored and to make their Paris all that their hearts desire. Ladies, engage your gigolos, by the dance, day, or week. Faces, manners and fees, to suit.'

Paul Carbone and François Spirito, two shady characters from Marseilles, are credited with the idea of starting a brothel specifically to serve foreign visitors. With Charles Martel as manager and his wife Marguerite (aka 'Martoune') as the legally required female manager, they opened Le Sphinx on Montparnasse's Boulevard Edgar Quinet in 1931.

In the traditional *maisons closes* (closed houses), clients purchased tokens from the management and used them to recompense the girls, but the Sphinx adopted the system of American nightclubs, and levied a 'cover charge' at the door. The system was explained in a brochure in half a dozen languages, the English section written by Henry Miller, who took payment 'in kind' with some of the establishment's *pensionnaires* (boarders), as the girls were called.

A discreet five-storey building in Art Deco style, it was identified by simple relief of a sphinx on the façade. Clients passed murals in Egyptian style by Kees van Dongen to enter a mirrored cabaret where a band played for dancing and a bar served cocktails. Air-conditioned, with lights that could be dimmed as the evening progressed, it resembled, said one admiring customer, the first-class lounge of a transatlantic liner – except that, strolling among the tables, were dozens of beautiful women wearing just high-heeled shoes. Periodically they paraded on stage to offer a better look. If someone wished to accompany one of them to the mirrored bedrooms upstairs, an elevator awaited.

The presence of the Mayor of Montparnasse and his wife at the gala opening established from the start that this was the acceptable face of the brothel business. It became a familiar stop on the celebrity grand tour. Cary Grant, Errol Flynn and Marlene Dietrich were among its regulars. A telephone booth was reserved for the use of journalists to report on the night's famous faces. When bandleader Duke Ellington paid a visit, his hosts urged him to choose a companion for the night. At first he demurred, but soon gave in. Reviewing the line-up on stage, he said, 'I'll take the three on the right.'

Although Napoleon I was sexually naive until Joséphine de Beauharnais took him in hand, he was also a soldier, and accepted the inevitability of prostitution. Sodomy had been legalized before he came to power in 1804 and he continued the process of decriminalizing sex, subject to restrictions which, significantly, were not religious or moral but legal and medical. Streetwalking was discouraged by a system of registration and medical supervision, and the licensing of brothels, known as *maisons de tolerance* (tolerated houses) or *maisons closes*. All prostitutes had to register with the police. Any working outside a brothel risked arrest and prison. All submitted to a weekly medical examination. Anyone infected with an STD was jailed until cured; a harsh but effective solution. To eradicate pimping, only a woman could manage a brothel. To the *dramatis personae* of the oldest profession was added another archetype, the manageress or madame, superficially amiable to clients but to her employees calculating and unsentimental. Clients paid her, and she in turn paid the wages, and provided food and lodging if women 'lived in'. 'Boyfriends' or 'protectors' (i.e. pimps), were excluded, and 'to live off immoral earnings' became a crime.

This rule didn't apply to the syndicates of businessmen and aristocrats who owned the brothels and took the profits. No shame was attached to such an investment. Guy de Maupassant's *The House of Madame Tellier*, published in 1885, calls the brothel of the title a valued amenity, patronized by 'respectable tradesmen, and young men in government or some other employ' who 'went there every evening about eleven o'clock, just as they would go to the club'. Tongue-in-cheek, Maupassant – a sexual athlete and *habitué* of Paris's *bordels* who died of syphilis contracted there – offers Mme Tellier's establishment as a model of good sense in matters of sex. 'The prejudice which is so violent and deeply rooted in large towns does not exist in the country places in Normandy. The peasant says "It is a paying-business" and he sends his daughter to keep an establishment of this character just as he would send her to keep a girls' school.'

In return for a toehold on respectability, the law demanded that brothels exercised discretion. Solid shutters must obscure what took place inside. The red lamp used in other countries was not permitted. Most establishments were identified simply by their address; Le 122 referred to 122 rue du Provence, Le Chabanais to the discreet House of All Nations on that street. Others affected the most bland of titles: At My Brother-in-Law's or My Sister's Place. Miss Molly's, directly opposite the Saint-Sulpice church, catered to the 50 per cent of Catholic priests who chafed at celibacy. In each case, only a slightly more prominent house number signified the correct address.

By 1810, Paris had 180 brothels, and within fifty years there were more than a thousand nationally. With legality came social acceptance. The itinerary of every visiting head of state included 'an evening with the President of the Sénat', but instead of a night of speeches and toasts, guests were conveyed to 12 rue Chabanais. The only hint that it housed the city's most gifted purveyors of pleasure was a sign on the restaurant opposite. 'What we serve,' it said, 'is as good as what you get across the road.'

The best brothels earned the title *maisons de fantasie* (houses of illusion). An evening at Le Chabanais was an adventure in sensuality. Its wardrobes contained costumes for nuns, brides, harem girls and ladies of the court from the time of Madame de Pompadour. Retired provincial administrators nostalgic for France's African colonies could request the Moorish room, with palm trees and a canvas panorama of desert scenes, the same one that provided a moving landscape outside the window of the simulated Orient Express sleeping car.

At top-drawer *bordels*, women were chosen for charm and intelligence as well as beauty. The same was true of the décor. At the Paris World Exposition of 1889, individual nations built separate pavilions containing displays of artwork and craft. The Japanese pavilion included a self-contained room filled with furniture, ceramics, metal work and textiles. After it won a prize, one of the investors bought the whole room and had it installed intact at Le Chabanais. Another added a suite in the style of Louis XVI, with porcelain medallions painted with plump pink nudes à la François Boucher. American expatriate Harry Crosby, nephew of financier J.P. Morgan, praised 'the Persian and the Russian and the Turkish and the Japanese and the Spanish rooms, and the bathroom with mirrored walls and mirrored ceilings, and the thirty harlots waiting in the salon'.

Water was filtered lest a speck of grit mar the clients' pleasure, and two elevators ensured against awkward encounters on the stairs. Each room had two entrances; the second, on a back corridor, fitted with a peephole, both for the management to keep an eye on what happened inside and for the benefit of voyeurs. When Salvador Dalí paid his first visit, the manageress, Madame Kelly, intuited that sex for the infantile young man took place most vividly in his imagination and let him loose in this corridor. A few hours later, he left in a daze, 'with enough', he wrote, 'to last me for the rest of my life in the way of accessories to furnish, in less than a minute, no matter what erotic reverie, even the most exacting'.

Prince Edward, later King Edward VII, liked to sit with cronies around a bath in which a girl bathed in champagne, and dip out the occasional glass. Le Chabanais obliged him by creating a copper bath decorated with dragons at each end. His obesity also complicated most sexual acts, so a cabinetmaker created a piece of furniture on which one or more women could recline at a height and position convenient to his royal horniness.

The best establishments boasted kitchens and wine cellars. Le 122's restaurant offered *boeuf à la ficelle* (beef fillet in broth), which gained something from being served by a waitress naked except for high heels, an apron and a gardenia in her hair. Eggs featured in the sexual fantasies of certain clients, either raw or, in a popular fetish, made into an omelette and slid sizzling onto their body.

The superficial elegance of Le Chabanais and other exclusive brothels hid a punishing regime. The cost of food and lodging was deducted from earnings, so the women were always in debt. Occasionally a client bought out a favourite, set her up as his mistress, sometimes in her own shop, and, on rare occasions, married her, but in general their future was bleak. Beating or even mutilating a prostitute was considered a misdemeanour at most. A textbook of the time asserted that 'what the criminal is to men, the prostitute is to women'. It also concluded that the skulls of prostitutes – and therefore their brains – were smaller than those of ordinary women, so however attractive they might be as sex objects, they had no more standing as sentient beings than a lapdog.

Paris brothels flourished throughout the German Occupation, the best becoming nightclubs for the high command. All this ended in 1946, when the Communist Party ran Marthe Richard, 'the French Mata Hari', as a candidate in the first post-war municipal elections. During the First World War she had spied for France. A wildly fictitious memoir, adapted as a film in 1937, made her a celebrity. In 1946, as the 'heroine of two wars', she was elected to the city council, despite accusations that she'd organized sex parties for Nazi officers and their cronies, and taken 300,000 francs to obtain the release of a convicted collaborator.

Among her campaign promises, shrewdly chosen by her backers, was one to close the brothels. Not only did it feed a national impulse towards penitence and moral regeneration, most people didn't patronize brothels, so could vote freely for their abolition. An additional plan, that the brothel buildings be refurbished as residences for returning soldiers, was equally attractive. Who could begrudge a young family their first home? Richard was elected and her propositions became law. But as most soldiers declined to begin their post-war lives in a whorehouse, all but a few of the buildings reverted to *hôtels de passe*, renting rooms by the hour to prostitutes who, since prostitution itself remained legal, continued working, but now on the street with pimps on the prowl and no medical supervision: the worst of all worlds.

Proprietors of the Sphinx and Le Chabanais inflicted what revenge they could on those politicians who, in the interests of political expediency, supported Marthe Richard but remained their best clients. At public auctions of furniture and fittings, they made a point of identifying the politicians and public figures who used them. The copper bath of Edward VII was bought by Salvador Dalí, who installed it in his suite at the hotel Le Meurice. Marthe Richard made no comment on the chaos inflicted by these clumsy attempts at social reform. At the end of her life, asked to what she attributed her longevity, she responded, thin-lipped, 'Abstinence.'

EXPLORING PARIS AFTER DARK

'Three matches, one by one, struck in the night,' wrote Jacques Prévert in one of his best-known poems. 'The first to see the whole of your face/ The second to see your eyes/ The last to see your mouth/ And the complete and utter darkness to remember them all/ While holding you in my arms.'

Prévert was a creature of the night. Darkness inspired his best work, including the lyrics for '*Les feuilles mortes*' (Autumn Leaves), which Joseph Kosma set to music the following year for the 1946 film Prévert also scripted, *Les Portes de la nuit* (The Gates of Night), a gaunt, despairing account of scores settled in the wake of the Occupation.

So filled is the Paris night with these resonances of history – with tales of lost and ancient loves, of violence, carnage, war and retribution – that successive city administrations have urged citizens to stay out after dark and enjoy them. Such initiatives have not always ended well. The latest dates from 1982, when François Mitterrand's innovative Culture Minister Jack Lang inaugurated the first Fête de la musique. Parisians were encouraged to spend the night in the streets, either listening to or performing music. The result was often cacophonous but the event soon became a fixture of the artistic calendar. Similar initiatives followed: a Fête du cinéma with cheap seats for all-night screenings; a Fête de la poésie, celebrating poetry and small press publishers.

In 2001, Mayor Bertrand Delanoë designated a night in early October as an annual Nuit Blanche or White Night. Shops, museums and theatres would be encouraged to stay open and citizens invited to roam the streets from dusk to dawn. Critics cavilled that white nights in Russia and northern Scandinavia were not 'declared' but took place naturally. From 11 June to 2 July, around St Petersburg, the sun hovers just below the horizon, bathing the city in pearly luminescence. Although similar conditions produce the same effect across Scandinavia, where it's called 'the midnight sun', Fyodor Dostoevsky's *Belye nochi* (White Nights) was the first book to record the introspection bordering on despair that ceaseless day can induce.

M. Delanoë's concept, loaded with incentives for people to stay up past their bedtime, was in line with other attempts to re-animate the streets which, after hours, were increasingly deserted. He even announced his intention to stay up and welcome in person anyone who cared to drop by the Hôtel de Ville. In 2002, an out-of-work computer technician turned up and, announcing he didn't like either homosexuals or politicians, stabbed him, fortunately not seriously. After that, a bodyguard accompanied the mayor at such events.

As the idea was picked up by Rome, Montreal, Toronto, Brussels, Madrid, Lima, Malaga, Taipei, Seoul and Leeds, Anne Hidalgo, one-time deputy to Delanoë, and his successor, made it an annual event. It accorded with her policy of removing cars from the city, encouraging bicycle use, filling public squares with 'urban forests' and reserving as many streets as possible for pedestrians. An artistic director was given €1.5 million to enliven the night with eye-catching spectacle. She promised to turn the city into 'a large exuberant garden, invested with unusual scenes, populated by rare forms and crossed by intriguing creatures'. Mayor Hidalgo assured the public that 'Parisians will throng the streets,' indifferent to the fact that many *quartiers* of Paris are largely unthrongable, if not downright hostile, and that some of those 'intriguing creatures' might mean one harm.

To make a White Night official deprives it of spontaneity. No Parisian should need a pretext to go out at night. Any evening, one can walk as Prévert did to the banks of the Seine, take a seat at one of the cafés that remain open until 2 a.m., and watch the moon over the Grand Palais or wait for that moment each hour when the Eiffel Tower comes alive with a million flickering lights. There will be music from the buskers who work the cafés on Place Dauphine, and perhaps one's eyes will meet those of another on the other side of the *terrasse* (the paved area outside a café). 'My God, a moment of bliss!' wrote Dostoevsky. 'Why, isn't that enough for a whole *lifetime*?'

WAYS
OF LIFE

PARISIANS AND THEIR POOLS

I n 1956, as cinemagoers in Britain and America enjoyed the spectacle of *The Ten Commandments*, *The King and I* and *Around the World in 80 Days*, those in Europe were transfixed by a modest tale of French fisherfolk. Roger Vadim's *Et Dieu … créa la femme* wouldn't reach English-speaking audiences until the following year, giving censors time to tone down the literal translation of its title, *And God Created Woman*, to the less controversial *And Woman Was Created*. They also removed some scenes in which Vadim showed off his immodest young wife, Brigitte Bardot, as she loafed, pouting and barely clothed, around the then-sleepy village of St Tropez.

Watching her, audiences outside France may have wondered why, despite the adjacent Mediterranean, nobody ever swam. But Vadim understood how the French regard their waters: not as their owner but as a lover. They admire, praise, contemplate, study, paint and photograph them. But swim? Not so much. You can tell what they expect from a seaside resort by the term they use to describe it: *station balnéaire*, from the Latin *statio* (to stare – literally 'to stand upright') and *balneum*, bath. According to one definition, it's 'a place by the sea, or any other place with baths fitted out for the reception of vacationers'. Swimming isn't mentioned.

Resorts faced with this prejudice against immersion resourcefully invented *Thalassothérapie*, a health treatment using products of the sea, and named for the Greek goddess who ruled it. A typical regime began with a battering from a stream of saltwater at fire-hose force, followed by a bath in lukewarm seawater mixed with powdered seaweed and other marine organics, an experience not unlike floating in gravy. After a shower and body massage, the client was laid out next to an Olympic-sized swimming pool and invited to contemplate an ocean view while soothing music and filtered sunlight lulled jangled nerves. One had absorbed as much of the ocean's bounty as someone swimming the English Channel, but never actually touched toe to wave – to the French, an ideal encounter with the sea.

In the 1920s and 1930s, when Germany could boast 1,360 public pools and Britain 800, Paris had a mere fifteen, and the entire country not many more. The most famous, Piscine Deligny, dating from 1796, floated on the Seine, in the very heart of the city, next to Place de la Concorde and the National Assembly. Essentially a barge with two pools in the middle, it served mostly as a café, although many celebrities enjoyed a dip. George Sand swam there, and the young Marcel Proust remembered his mother enjoying its waters. On its shady terrace, partly built of timbers taken from *La Dorade*, the boat that brought the body of Napoleon I from St Helena for reburial, ladies of leisure met friends for tea and weary men-about-town enjoyed an *aperitif*. From to time, a couple might exchange a glance. If anything came of it, they could retire to one of the changing rooms.

Nobody considered swimming in the Seine itself. An 1844 survey found its waters '*sale, trouble, souvent fétide et malsaine*' (dirty, cloudy, often foul-smelling and unhealthy). Rather than risk it, the 1900 Olympic Games chose the Deligny for its swimming events, even though the filtering was inadequate. The Seine deteriorated further, and in 1923 swimming in it was made illegal, following the death of young novelist Raymond Radiguet, who succumbed to typhoid fever after doing so. The Deligny limped along with its dubious sanitation until the German Occupation of 1940–44, when the Wehrmacht and Luftwaffe officers, for whom the use of all Paris's pools – like its best brothels – was reserved, insisted on a state-of-the-art upgrade.

By the 1960s, the Deligny, having survived a fire and collisions with passing freight-hauling *chaland* barges, was a floating disco and bar, popular as a gay hangout, comparable to the steam baths or *hammams* of the Marais. A member of the National Assembly complained that while crossing the bridge on his way to a sitting, he was distracted from loftier thoughts by the sight of nude toy boys sunbathing below. Rather than suggesting he avert his eyes, the owners screened off the terrace, but these indignities were too much for the timbers that had borne the bones of Napoleon, and during the night of Thursday, 8 July 1993, the Deligny, possibly from shame, sank ignominiously into the mud.

Its place had already been usurped by the more durable Piscine Molitor. Built from concrete rather than wood, and sited by the river but not actually on it, the Molitor, inaugurated in 1929, was designed in the Art Deco manner. Circular portholes and stained-glass windows suggested transatlantic ocean liners, then the measure of leisure style. Three tiers of shops, cafés, promenades and blue-doored dressing rooms ('the scene of much dalliance', noted the owners, with a wink) made it the most popular swimming pool in Paris. As its first Honorary Lifeguard, it hired American swimmer and three-times-gold Olympic champion Johnny Weissmuller, later famous for his movie performances as Tarzan.

For sixty years, its indoor and outdoor pools (one of which was frozen in winter for skating) drew millions of bathers, attracted by its 'beaches' with real sand along the edge of the water. In 1946, designer Louis Réard chose the Molitor to launch his pioneering two-piece swimsuit named the Bikini, after the atoll where the Americans had tested a nuclear weapon four days earlier. Regular models refused to wear the abbreviated outfit, small enough, he boasted, to fit in a matchbox (though by today's standards positively voluminous). Micheline Bernardini, a former nude dancer at the Casino de Paris, took the job, and entered history.

Derelict by 1989, its fittings looted, walls covered in graffiti, the Molitor was briefly saved by its designation as a national monument, but further deterioration led to its almost total demolition. Some features were incorporated into a hotel, but while the pool is still in use, the blue doors to its banks of once-notorious changing rooms now open, disappointingly, on to bare concrete.

Today, Paris has thirty-nine public pools, one named for Josephine Baker, who was not known for her aquatic expertise. The most obscure pool, commemorating swimming coach Suzanne Berlioux, lies three levels below what used to be the city's food market, Les Halles. A glass wall provides a view of the pool and the space that encloses it, which, because of its humid atmosphere, has the languid tropical atmosphere of a jungle pool.

Each summer, the city dumps sand at a few points along the stone-paved banks of the Seine to create *Paris plages* (Paris beaches). Parasols provide shelter from the sun, concession stands sell drinks and ice-cream, and the city stages concerts, film screenings, games for children and even a dance. *Brumisateurs* fill the air with a fine and cooling mist, but on no account is one permitted to swim. Nor would anyone wish to, once they hear about the chemicals and detritus dumped in the river – not to mention the crocodiles; former pets that, according to legend, flourish in the subterranean creeks and storm-water channels flowing into it.

It's promised that all this will change. By 2025, the city plans to have three open-air swimming areas accessible from the river bank. 'When people see athletes swimming in the Seine with no health problems,' predicted the Deputy Mayor at the time of writing, Pierre Rabadan, 'they'll be confident themselves to start going back in the Seine.' Or perhaps, as now, they will just lie in the sun and watch.

Incidentally, the Seine is not alone among France's great rivers in being unsuitable for swimming. The Loire has been closed to swimmers since nineteen children drowned in 1969. The Rhône and Saône are likewise out of bounds, particularly around the city of Lyon. Swimming in the Rhine is permitted, but only on the Swiss side of the border. As for the Garonne, which passes through Bordeaux and Toulouse, high and low tides, dangerous currents and the occasional large merchant ship put it decisively off limits also. Best stick to the *Paris plages*.

THE LATE LAMENTED

THE FRENCH AND FUNERALS

On most days during the 1930s, a few soberly dressed individuals could be seen in Montparnasse's Café du Dôme, lingering over a cold coffee or the dregs of a beer while scanning the intersection of boulevards Raspail and Montparnasse. They were watching for funerals heading to the nearby cemetery. If a cortège appeared, they hurriedly settled their bill and joined those walking solemnly behind the hearse. Similar scenes were repeated at Père-Lachaise, Montmartre and other Parisian cemeteries. This wasn't out of respect. Traditionally, after the burial, bereaved families invited mourners, whether they knew them or not, to a café for a meal.

France is no different to most countries in making more fuss of someone after they're dead than they ever did in life. When a person is placed in the Panthéon, the highest honour the nation can bestow, the ceremonial is elaborate. For the internment of Resistance hero Jean Moulin in December 1964, a coffin was taken from a boat on the Seine and placed on a Second World War tank which crawled up Boulevard St Michel, followed by members of the Resistance and their families carrying burning torches. As they passed each building on this busiest of avenues, all its lights went out. An honour guard of generals stood by the coffin all night, and the next afternoon André Malraux delivered one of the most stirring orations of modern times: 'Welcome, general of the armies of the night, at the head of your dreadful retinue ...'

Parisian cemeteries are filled with monuments to the great of the past, as well as those who considered themselves great, and had the money to leave that impression. Charles Pigeon (1838–1915), believing the invention of a gasoline lamp entitled him to celebrity treatment even in death, topped his family tomb in Montparnasse cemetery with life-sized bronze effigies of himself and his wife in bed. The tomb, sufficiently spacious to accommodate eighteen family members, has its own angel guardian and is wired for electric light. Mme Pigeon, looking resigned, wears a nightgown, but M. Pigeon is fully clothed in frock coat and cravat, and, alert for inspiration even in death, has a pen and notebook in hand.

Figures in the arts seldom leave behind such flamboyant monuments, although their funerals often make up for it. That for Jean Cocteau's lover and protégé Raymond Radiguet (1903–23) was designed by couturier Coco Chanel. The jazz band from Cocteau's cabaret Boeuf sur le Toit occupied the front row of the church, and a horse-drawn hearse carried the white coffin covered in red roses, the mourners walking behind in the pouring rain.

Radiguet lies in Père-Lachaise under a modest slab of grey marble – not far from Oscar Wilde (1854–1900) who, though he died destitute and in disgrace, is commemorated by a massive sphinx in Aztec style, chiselled in 1914 by Jacob Epstein from 20 tonnes of Derbyshire granite. Traditionally, a sphinx has the head of a man but the body of a lion, which Epstein took as a hint to give his figure genitals of proportions appropriate to a king of beasts. In 1961, two ladies – British, naturally, and driven by what dark impulse one can only imagine – chiselled them off. Since then, thick Perspex has prevented admirers from getting too close to the memorial, whether to deface it or add lipsticked kisses. The whereabouts of his missing appendages remain unknown, and the current curator dismisses the rumour that successive occupants of his job use them for a paperweight as complete and utter balls.

Oscar's lost gonads are just one of the attractions that lure three million people a year to Paris's largest – 43ha – bone yard, built on land acquired from François d'Aix de la Chaise, aka Père (Father) Lachaise, confessor to Louis XIV. Many come to see the grave of rock star Jim Morrison (1943–71), lead singer of the Doors: so many, in fact, that it's now fenced off from fans eager to deface it or deposit flowers, incense, bad poetry and the occasional joint.

Notwithstanding Andrew Marvell's contention that 'the grave's a fine and private place/ But none I think do there embrace', many of Père-Lachaise's monuments have erotic overtones. More testicular legends lurk around the lavish tomb in which the famous lovers Héloïse and Abelard are supposed, erroneously, to be buried. Abelard was castrated by the guardian of his lover Héloïse. It's customary in some circles to place a token on a grave to signify your visit. In this case most people choose a pebble but one comic left a pair of walnuts.

There are even more visitors, most of them women, to the memorial for Victor Noir. This obscure journalist was only twenty-one in 1870 when an assassin cut him down in the full flower of – if the life-sized bronze figure sprawled across his tomb is anatomically accurate – a well-endowed manhood. Tradition holds that if a woman straddles the figure and rubs her crotch against his, she will become pregnant, win a lover or, at worse, enjoy a pleasurable *frisson*. Whatever their reasons, generations of visitors have polished that point of the statue to a gleam.

A recent director of Père-Lachaise lamented the decline in such ostentatious memorials as that to Victor Noir. 'Vanity has been consigned to the cupboard and sobriety is now the fashion,' he wrote. 'As the curator of a cemetery known for its exceptional monuments, I consider this "funerary timidity" to be rather regrettable. Père-Lachaise would not be this remarkable place if megalomania had not one day pushed the most fortunate to have tombs built in the image of their bloated pride.' It's possible, of course, that he was prejudiced, belonging as he did to a family of memorial stonemasons.

Lately, Père-Lachaise has taken on new life as a tourist attraction, popular even with ecologists, who value it as a sanctuary for feral cats, foxes, bats and, no doubt, in season, the occasional werewolf. Since its gardeners use no pesticides, all kinds of wild flowers and plants flourish there. How long before some enterprising *opiomane* (opium addict) remembers the story in Claude Farrère's *Fumée d'Opium* about the old soldier who, pining for the opium he learned to enjoy while posted to France's Asian colonies, takes a job as watchman in an overgrown cemetery where he can manufacture his own from its poppies?

A visit to Père-Lachaise and a stroll through its leafy alleys remains one of the most unusual and illuminating experiences Paris has to offer. It's not only the graves of celebrities that intrigue most. One of the most enigmatic monuments is that of one Fernand Arbelot, who died in 1942 after an apparently unremarkable life as head of a Paris bank. It clearly paid well, since he could afford to commission the life-sized bronze figure that adorns the tomb he shares with his wife. He's shown lying on his back and holding before his face a mask of ... who? His wife? A lover? Man or woman? Himself? The sex isn't clear, and now never will be. What does the figure celebrate? Love lost? Love that endures? Not love at all, but

something more abstract, and less finite? Torment or consolation? The message on the tomb doesn't help. It reads simply, 'They were amazed at the beautiful journey which led them to the end of life.' To whomever it belonged, that face will be before his eyes as long as Paris survives. Envy him this eternal and ageless enigma.

LEAGUES, MILES AND THE FOOT OF HERCULES
THE FIGHT FOR METRICATION

On rue de Vaugirard, in the 6th arrondissement, opposite the Palais du Luxembourg, now the home of the Senate, you will find, tucked in under the colonnade, embedded in a wall and almost invisible from the street, a monument to one of the most significant and far-reaching achievements of the French Revolution.

A modest pediment in Roman style, sculpted from local limestone, shelters a slab of marble into which two brass pins are set and, between them, a line, divided into tenths. The word 'MÈTRE', chiselled into the marble in a discreet sans serif face, declares unequivocally its standing as a constant. Let the rest of the world change. The metre is set in stone.

Sixteen of these *mètres étalons* (standard metres) were installed around Paris in 1796 and 1797 but this is the only one still in its original location. They were placed at shoulder height so that people could measure their arm or a yardstick against it and carry a practical comparison back to their workshop or market.

On the eve of the Revolution, an estimated quarter of a million different units of measurement were in use. Depending on where you lived, distances were calculated in miles, yards, inches, feet, perches or roods, in leagues, ells and arpents; areas in acres or hectares; speeds at sea in knots and depths in fathoms; weights in tons, hundredweights, pounds, ounces, pennyweights and grains; quantities in dozens or gross; money in francs, ecus, pounds, shillings, pence, farthings, half-crowns and guineas.

In an added complication, measurements of the same name differed between countries, even regions. In northern France, Jules Verne's *Twenty Thousand Leagues Under the Sea* represented a voyage of roughly 60,000km, but in Provence, measured according to the local definition of a league, almost twice that. Few had any rational basis. The British based the foot, according to legend, on the length of the foot of Hercules. It was shorter than the French *pied*, just as the British pound was worth less than the French *livre*. The length of a yard also differed from country to country – or rather king to king, since successive rulers decreed it should be the distance from the tip of their nose to an upraised thumbnail at the end of an extended arm.

Although it gave no consolation to the people of France who had to master its intricacies, metrication at least had a rational basis, rooted in science. In the midst of the Revolution, astronomers Jean Baptiste Joseph Delambre and Pierre Méchain spent seven years painstakingly establishing the exact distance from the north pole to the equator. Once they had a figure, the commissioners appointed by the Academy of Sciences announced grandly, 'We fix the unit of measurement at the ten-millionth part of a quarter of the meridian and we call it mètre.' On 22 July 1799, objects of platinum representing the mètre and kilogram were ceremonially placed in the National Archives and on 10 December 1799 a new law confirmed their status as the sole standards for measuring length and mass in France.

Establishing the new system was one thing; getting people to observe it another. Metrication wouldn't be legally adopted in France until 1875, and it took more than a century for such bastions of tradition as Australia to see the light. After the United States chose decimal currency in 1792, Thomas Jefferson intended to make the new nation fully metric, and asked the French for copies of the standard kilogram and metre. These were entrusted to botanist Joseph Dombey, but en route to New York his ship was blown off course and he was captured by pirates from the Caribbean island of Montserrat, where he died in captivity a year later. As a result, it would take more than a century for metrication to become United States' national policy, with still no sign of it being put into practice.

However widely metrication is accepted, vestiges of the old system will remain embedded in the language. The 'grain of truth' referred to in the proverb isn't a seed but the grain of the Troy weight system - $\frac{1}{7000}$ of a pound - by which gold is measured. Carats remain the unit of weight for diamonds, and it's a penny rather than a cent that we offer for someone's thoughts. Likewise, it will always be 'full fathom five' that a father lies in *The Tempest*, a pound of flesh that Shylock will demand in *The Merchant of Venice* and at the rate of 'half a league, half a league, half a league onward' that the Light Brigade in Tennyson's poem rides into the valley of death. The heavy footfall of Hercules isn't easily erased.

SERVICE COMPRIS
TO TIP OR NOT TO TIP?

Until twenty years ago in France, one tipped for anything that exhibited skill: the usherette who guided you to a theatre or cinema seat, the *poissonnière* in the fish market who boned your sole, the butcher who trimmed a *gigot* or prepared a chicken. To jog your memory, a glass with a few coins stood by the cash register, and the usherette gave a suggestive swish to the coins in the cloth bag at her waist.

Adding an obligatory 15 per cent for service was meant to end this practice, but in many cases it simply complicated it further. In Diane Johnson's *Le Divorce*, one of the best novels about the differences between French and American manners, Roxy and Isabel, American sisters who have lived in Paris and understand its etiquette, take their Californian family to an expensive restaurant where Isabel has eaten with her wealthy French lover, Edgar:

> At the end, Roger, paying the bill, said, 'The tip is included.'
> 'You leave something anyhow,' I said.
> 'No, that's the whole point of having the tip included. I think it's a very rational system,' Roger said.
> 'Maybe twenty francs,' Roxy agreed with me.
> 'Fuck it, fifteen per-cent has already been added,' Roger said.
> 'Maybe in a simple place, you add, Isabel, but here, when you've already paid a fortune for dinner...' said Margeeve.
> 'Nearly seven hundred dollars, if I may say so,' Roger said, his voice trembling a little.
> 'I have some tens.' Roxy scrambled in her purse and gave three *dix-franc* coins to me. I put them on the little plate with the bill. Roger's jaw clenched, and Chester looked embarrassed. I knew Edgar would leave about a hundred francs in these circumstances, but who would listen to me?

It's a scene most Paris residents have experienced with friends from overseas. To understand tipping in France, one needs to go back to an era when servants performed most of the duties of hospitality. They were paid little, if at all: some worked just for room and board. A visitor who wished to reward them but not to appear patronizing might, on leaving, slip something into the servant's hand, explaining '*C'est pour vous*' (This is for you), making it clear that it wasn't charity but specifically for services rendered - or say '*Pour un boire*' (Have a drink on me). In some circles, a tip is still called *un pourboire*.

But why tip more if the restaurant is expensive? It's a question of expectations. What, in the house of rich people, would be considered generous? To tip a few coins when the servant is accustomed to more would be insulting. Again, the amount is less important than the message.

Even if the waiter in a café receives the legal wage and enjoys the same benefits as every taxpayer, he or she is still doing you a personal service. It's not the 'service' we tip but the 'personal'. For this reason, people often leave a few coins on the table or tell the waiter, 'Keep the rest.' It acknowledges the fact that the entire 15 per cent will not necessarily remain with that person. Restaurants regard the tip as belonging to everyone, not just to those who interact directly with the customer. The kitchen staff, the sommelier, even madame at the cash register - all expect a share. If a customer tips less than expected, or not at all, everyone suffers. In luxury resorts, it's not unusual for a restaurant to refuse to seat diners who don't guarantee to spend - and, more important, tip - lavishly; the management of such places make this a condition of accepting a booking. Not long ago, a wealthy Italian was pursued into the car park in St Tropez by a waiter protesting that he'd been left a €500 tip, about 10 per cent of the bill, rather than the 'customary' 20 per cent. Rude, yes. Arrogant even. But one can see his point.

SELLING THE PAST

GOING, GOING, GONE ...

F
ew nations set such store by the past as the French. They see no
special virtue in modernity. The old is treasured, tradition embraced,
the *patrimoine* or cultural heritage held in high esteem.

A *brocante* is proof at its simplest of this respect. A street market for
second-hand goods, its name derives from *broc-a-brac*, origin of the English
'bric-a-brac'. Both describe the sort of things sold in such markets: items too
interesting or worthwhile to throw away, but too recent or trivial to be called
antiques; often dismissed as 'junk' but embraced by others as 'collectibles'.
Outside France, you hear such events described as *marchés aux puces* – flea
markets (or swap meets in some countries) – but French merchants shun
this phrase with its suggestion that their stock is infested with vermin.
They prefer variations on the verb *chiner*, meaning to buy and sell, and call
themselves *chineurs*.

Two permanent *brocantes*, Porte de Clignancourt and Porte de
Vanves, lie at opposite edges of Paris, the first to the north, the other south-
west. Porte de Vanves, occupying a few streets around the inner ring road
or *périphérique*, is the place for serious buyers, the professionals' choice.
Clignancourt, sometimes called Porte de Ouen, is on a different scale. Almost
a suburb in itself, it has paved alleys and permanent shops. On summer
weekends, the surrounding streets become infested with sellers of T-shirts,
dubious electronics and worse. Seasoned buyers leave it to the tourists. But
Clignancourt looks the way a film producer thinks a market should, and so
in Woody Allen's 2011 film *Midnight in Paris,* it's there that Owen Wilson's
visiting American writer goes with his odious in-laws, and is beguiled by a
pretty French girl selling antique Cole Porter records. No *real* movie star
would be seen there, but one does occasionally encounter Catherine Deneuve
at Porte de Vanves or browsing rural *brocantes* near her country home; just
another *brocanteuse,* enjoying the atmosphere and the day.

In addition to the year-round *brocantes*, pop-up markets appear
– mostly in summer and autumn – in streets and open spaces around the
suburbs. To suggest the vendors are amateurs and the event a community
effort, the municipal councils that license them attach such reassuring
names as *Grand balai* (Big Sweep-out), *Vide grenier* (Attic Emptier), *Grand
braderie* (Major Clearance) or *Marché pour tous* (Market for Everyone), but

most sellers are semi-professionals and the syndicates that run the markets charge to take part.

Occasionally a brocante will style itself *Marché antiquaire*, a warning for experienced *chineurs* to stay away. Technically, an antique must be more than 100 years old, but the definition is subject to infinite variability. Labels like *antiquaire* or *antique* can signify over-priced stock of dubious authenticity. Rating themselves above mere *brocanteurs*, *antiquaires* often set up tent-like marquees which they fit out as a shop with a few items of furniture and some *bibelots* (knickknacks). Taking a seat behind a suspiciously pristine desk in Louis XVI style, they open a copy of *Connoisseur* magazine and leaf through it, apparently indifferent, but alert for clients. The moment anyone shows the faintest interest, they are at his or her side, inviting them to just '... *feel* that embroidery, all original, I assure you ... And try this chair. What princes, even kings have sat here ...?'

Thrift shops on the British model, using high street shopfronts to sell used goods for charity, don't exist in France. The nearest equivalent is the *Dépôt vente* or commission shops selling used couture clothing. Supposedly, people place items with them for sale on commission, but in fact they are

second-hand stores specializing in high-fashion items; not only clothing but handbags, costume jewellery and shoes. For women on a budget, they represent their best chance of being able to wear Prada, Dior or St Laurent.

The remainder of the second-hand trade is dominated by Emmaus, a self-help co-operative set up in 1949 by Catholic priest and Capuchin friar Abbé Pierre after a particularly grim winter. Resourcefully, the Abbé bypassed the standard nickel-and-dime funding channels and approached celebrities and show business for help. Among those who assisted was Alain Bernardin, who volunteered his Crazy Horse cabaret for a fund-raiser. Emmaus, now international, operates permanent *brocantes* all over France, run by volunteers, many of them formerly homeless, who are employed collecting and refurbishing items for resale.

Late in the twentieth century, after generations of dealing with scholars and insiders alone, collecting boomed. Television programmes such as *Antiques Roadshow* put a price tag on everything from baseball cards to Gutenberg Bibles. In Paris, most items changed hands at the Hôtel Drouot (pronounced 'drew-o'). Established in 1852, it's the world's oldest auction house, although, unlike Sotheby's, Christie's and similar venues elsewhere, it doesn't sell on its own account but leases space to *commissaires-priseurs* – independent auctioneers who gather the items and conduct sales. The Drouot's element of rough-and-tumble can disconcert anyone accustomed to the sobriety of London and New York salerooms. *Commissaires-priseurs* are showmen, inclined to strut and grandstand. Buyers seldom stay for the whole sale, so there's an ebb and flow of people leaving and arriving, interrupted by shouts of '*Adjugé!*' (Sold!) and by applause. Occasionally, there's drama. The French government has the right, when an item of special historical or cultural interest appears, to pre-empt the sale, paying the hammer price but claiming the article for the nation. To the dealer who expected to sell a purchase at a profit, such news can be catastrophic.

It's to the suburban *brocante*, however, that the real connoisseur gravitates. As in many aspects of French life, there's a ritual to attendance, a sense of affirming a tradition. One doesn't go too early, since people are still setting up, and there are always a few professionals who will shoulder you aside to get at cartons even before they're opened. Nor should you wait until mid-afternoon, known in the trade as *l'heure du musée*, when people, after digesting their lunch, load the kids into their prams and go for a stroll. Blocking the paths between stalls, they never buy anything, but tend to rummage, commenting all the time 'Look at this, Jules. Remember? Our first flat?' Looking at the price, they yelp '€50? You're *joking!*', as if the vendors weren't sitting impassively a few metres away.

The best time to visit is late morning, when sellers are thinking about lunch. Perhaps the wife and daughter are unfolding the card table, setting out a baguette, salad in a Tupperware bowl, pâté, a bottle of wine. Then you hold up the €50 item and say '€30 for this?'

'Yes, sure,' they say vaguely, taking your money. 'And listen... You don't happen to have a corkscrew, do you?' And for that moment, you are part of the community, a citizen of the *brocante*; just another *chineur*.

ROLAND GARROS AND THE RED GAME

Tennis weaves through France's history like few other sports, though the original barely resembles today's cannonball game. Called Royal or Real Tennis in England and *Jeu de paume* in France, it was played indoors, with balls of cork, and on a court more like that used for squash, but with a sloped-roof shed, called a penthouse, running along one side. One could hit the ball directly over the net to an opponent or run it along the roof, hoping it would bounce off at an awkward angle, in what was known as a hazard.

In 1415, the dauphin, heir apparent to Charles VI of France, intending to mock England's King Henry V for a youth wasted in idleness and sport, sent a gift of tennis balls, an insult which, if William Shakespeare is to be believed, goaded him into invading France. In *Henry V*, young Hal responds to the insult with a stinging return. 'When we have match'd our rackets to these balls,/ We will, in France, by God's grace, play a set/ Shall strike his father's crown into the hazard.'

Tennis was a gentleman's game, and most chateaux had a court. In June 1789, a delegation of commoners summoned to the Palace of Versailles by Louis XVI was barred from a meeting to which aristocrats and churchmen were admitted. Furious, they reconvened in the royal tennis court, the largest space they could find, and, in the famous Oath of the Tennis Court, swore to overturn the monarchy. Less than four years later, Louis and his queen, Marie Antoinette, were dead on the guillotine.

Once modern tennis replaced the classic game, France rose to dominate the sport, led by such players as Suzanne Lenglen, known as *La Divine* (The Goddess), who pioneered tennis for women, and the 'Four Musketeers' – Jacques Brugnon, Jean Borotra (aka 'The Bounding Basque'), Henri Cochet (aka 'The Magician') and René Lacoste (aka 'The Crocodile') – who swept both singles and doubles titles. Lacoste was among the first athletes to accept sponsorship. A sportswear manufacturer exploited his nickname by embroidering that reptile on all its products, creating a line of clothing still world-famous.

Colour television made the red clay courts of the Stade Roland-Garros in Paris as instantly recognizable as the green grass of Wimbledon or the blue court surfaces of Australia and the United States. Although the 'clay' isn't clay at all but brick dust only a few centimetres deep spread over a bed of limestone, the French, by choosing a surface that retained a sense of the tropics, once again favoured poetry over the practical. There is drama in the red earth of the south. If Wimbledon's lawns are redolent of cucumber sandwiches and strawberries and cream, the clay of Roland-Garros brings a whiff of Provençal heat and the scent of wild thyme. Wimbledon is David Hockney; Roland-Garros is Pablo Picasso.

Visitors assume that Roland Garros, to have had the complex named for him, must have excelled in sports. In fact he was an aviator, the first man to fly across the Mediterranean, and inventor of a machine gun which, firing through the blades of a propellor, transformed aerial warfare. Paradoxically, he fell victim to his own invention, shot down during the last days of the First World War.

Small, dark, with a dashing moustache, Garros cycled, played football, rugby and tennis, and raced the cars of his friend Ettore Bugatti. He was also an accomplished pianist, and a familiar figure at the fashionable salons of Paris. At one of these he met American dancer Isadora Duncan, who performed to his playing of Chopin and invited him to escort her back to her hotel. They paused in the Place de la Concorde as the alert sounded for an air raid, and she danced for him alone in the empty square as anti-aircraft batteries roared and searchlights probed the sky overhead. 'He applauded me,' she wrote, 'sitting on the edge of a fountain, his melancholy black eyes shining with the fire of the rockets which fell and exploded not far from us. Shortly after, the Angel of Heroes seized him and carried him away.'

The poet and artist Jean Cocteau loved Garros, though it's not clear whether they were lovers. Garros did take him for night flights over Paris,

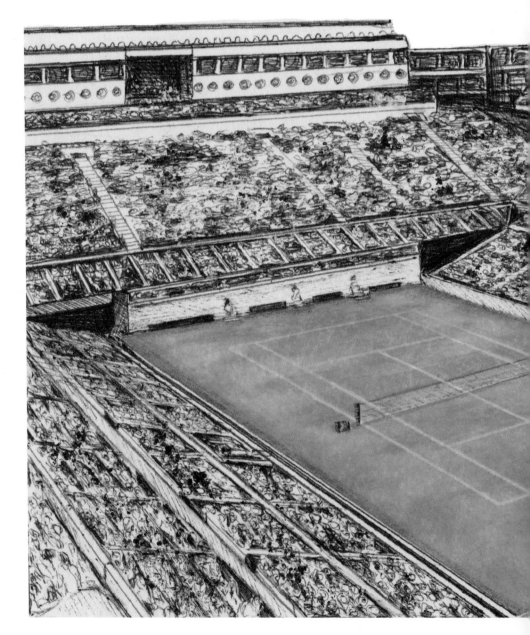

an experience that inspired Cocteau to poetry. 'He flies as he breathes,' he wrote. Garros was also mourned by Émile Lesieur, a school friend and fellow pilot who became an important figure in French sports. It was Lesieur who spontaneously decreed that the new tennis centre, constructed in 1928 to defend what was, at the time, France's overwhelming superiority in the sport, should bear Garros's name – though, since French law requires anything named for an individual to be hyphenated, both the stadium and the French Open contested there take place in the name of 'Roland-Garros'.

MÉTRO, BOULOT, DODO
LEARNING TO LOVE THE MÉTRO

I n the 1938 film *Algiers*, Hedy Lamarr, a tourist in that north African city, flirts with gangster Charles Boyer, doomed to remain a fugitive inside the Casbah, its slum district, or die in the streets outside.

'Do you know what you remind me of?' he asks her. 'The Métro. You're all silk, and you jingle when you walk, and yet with all that *chi chi* you make me think of the Métro. Isn't that funny? And *frites*, and coffee on the boulevard.'

Métro, boulot, dodo (Métro, job, sleep), the mantra of the Paris commuter, signals the importance of the city's transport network to its citizens. Paris was the first city to call its underground railway 'Métro', a name other cities from Moscow to Shanghai, have copied. Moscow's stations are more palatial and New York's IRT has inspired more cultural gems, notably Duke Ellington's 'Take the "A" Train', but no other system of rapid transit has accumulated such a treasury of romance. Nor, to exiles, is any sound more evocative of Paris than that squeal of its wheels as it takes a bend and the murmur of the air driven before it as it approaches a station.

The Paris Métro also breathes its own perfume. An actual fragrance, it's called Madeleine, a cocktail of synthetic vanilla, jasmine, lily, citrus and rose that's sprayed onto platforms, staircases and ticket halls at the rate of 1.5 tonnes a month. An earlier scent, Françine, tried to go organic with natural plant extracts, but eucalyptus, lavender and mint were no match for the effluvia of a working city, augmented pungently by the homeless who hide out there by night.

The Métro embraced eccentricity from the moment it opened in 1900. Tasked with designing a style of entrance that would suit every station on the network, Hector Guimard used the flowing vegetal curves of Art Nouveau to create a standard arch in which uprights reminiscent of giant alien plants were surmounted by eye-like lamps of a baleful orange/red. Two more sets of tendrils branched out to enclose and support a medallion in which the word '*Métropolitain*' quivered in a typeface just as exotic. Opponents compared his porticos of verdigris metal and frosted glass to the wings of bats, and the effect of his bulbous lamps to moon-dwellers looming over cowering commuters, but its use of pre-fabricated cast iron made the

system cheap as well as distinctive, so the city fathers, grumbling, gave in, and his design was soon unforgettably associated with Paris.

For its first century, the Métro was over-run with uniformed *fonctionnaires* of its controlling body, the Régie autonome des transports Parisiens (RATP). A humourless individual would sell you a ticket at the *guichet*, another would clip it as you descended to the platform, where his colleagues watched closely in case you tried to squeeze past the electric gate that swung shut each time a hoot announced the arrival of a train. Aiming to replicate the culture that existed above ground, including its social distinctions, the Métro even had first and second class cars. Despite protests from RATP, which charged 50 per cent extra for first-class tickets, and from pensioners and the disabled who bought them to be sure of a seat in its half-empty cars, first class was discontinued in 1981.

With its abolition, the Métro began to change. Electric barriers were dismantled. Ticket machines appeared. Staff also dwindled, until the system appeared to run itself – literally so on the newest lines. These days, there's seldom anyone behind the *guichet*. Vending machines sell tickets which are fed into electronic gates. At platform level, glass barriers open and close automatically, guiding us into spotless modern cars. Their drivers' cabins are empty. These trains have minds of their own – or no minds at all.

Over the years, many platforms among the Métro's almost 300 stations have been re-designed. Jules Verne inspired the décor at Arts et Métiers, the station closest to the museum of technology. Since 1994, copper has sheathed the walls, evoking Captain Nemo's submarine, the *Nautilus*, from *Twenty Thousand Leagues Under the Sea*. Auguste Rodin's *The Thinker* and his statue of Honoré de Balzac greet passengers alighting at Varenne for the nearby Musée Rodin. The tiles lining Concorde, above which the French royal family were guillotined, spell out the text of the Declaration of the Rights of Man. The Odéon station, excavated under the former home of Georges Jacques Danton, features a bust of the revolutionary firebrand executed in 1794. It may seem unfeeling to display just the head of a man decapitated on the guillotine but Danton wouldn't have minded. Mounting the scaffold, he told the assistant executioner, 'Don't forget to show my head to the people. It's well worth seeing.'

Few stations are more lavishly decorated than Louvre–Rivoli, which boasts copies of statues from the museum above, ranging from Egyptian kings to the Venus de Milo. Traditionally, the Métro is off-limits to graffiti artists, known as 'taggers', but in April 1991 a collective called VEP, led by a man with the *nom de bombe* Oeno, in collaboration with others signing themselves Stem and Gary, hid in unused tunnels until trains stopped at 1 a.m., then lavishly defaced Louvre-Rivoli. Their spray-painted signatures and abstract squiggles constituted, they announced, 'a veritable declaration of war' against the RATP.

The uproar was predictable. RATP called down hellfire on the vandals who attacked these (albeit facsimile) masterpieces with *bombes de peinture*. But the indignation didn't take root. Instead, editorials and op-ed pieces in the more thoughtful newspapers suggested Oeno and his team were simply redressing an imbalance. Didn't the art of the twenty-first century also deserve to be heard? Hadn't the Impressionists displayed similar impatience when they boycotted the established Salon and held their own *Salon des refusés*? The debate continued all week. Critics who hadn't travelled by Métro since primary school (grade school) now strolled the Louvre-Rivoli platform, less commuters than connoisseurs. In salons where no reference to any painter more recent than Poussin had been permitted for generations, dinner guests compared Jef Aérosol to Jean-Michel Basquiat, and argued the rival abilities of Speedy Graphito and Blek le Rat.

Then the fun was over. RATP cleaners went through the station, scouring the walls and sculptures. Journalists returned to tracking the sexual indiscretions of the president. But a point had been made. In December 1991, the new Minister of Cultural Affairs, Jack Lang, invited the taggers who had attacked the Métro to demonstrate their work as part of an art fair in La Défense, the ultra-modern business district on the outskirts of Paris. Graffiti had joined the establishment. And no Métro station has suffered a raid since.

In 2006, the Métro adopted the slogan '*Aimer le ville*' (Love the city). The accompanying logo, featuring a line resembling the route of the Seine as it flows through Paris, echoes a woman's face, upraised as for a kiss. Although the new Métro may have no brain, it still possesses a heart.

THE FRENCH AND NATURISM

'**I**s it true,' asks an American adolescent in the film *Home Alone* as he packs for a Christmas holiday in France, 'that French babes don't shave their pits?'

'Some don't,' admits his friend.

'But they got nude beaches?'

'Not in the winter,' the other reminds him glumly.

On the question of 'pits' and body hair, a 2006 survey found that 83 per cent of French women shaved their legs, 73 per cent their armpits and 54 per cent their bikini line. This had not always been the case. Before the Second World War, body hair was ubiquitous. American manufacturers of nylon stockings and depilatory cream are to blame for the change. Returning GIs brought news of the hirsute condition of French women, alerting them to a tempting new market.

The hairless 'Brazilian' style of pubic hair barbering has yet to catch on in France, except among sex workers and women who perform *en déshabillé*. Among the latter are the dancers of the Crazy Horse cabaret, Paris's premiere nude dance show. Its founder, Alain Bernardin, insisted that all his girls be between 1.66m and 1.72m tall, identically proportioned and shaved. He varied the rule only for what became the show's popular opening number, 'God Save Our Bare Skins', in which the dancers did close order drill in tall bearskin helmets, leather boots and harness, but otherwise nude. To emphasize that their physical features, from eyes to crotch, lined up precisely, Bernardin dictated the exceptional provision of pubic triangles, which, like the moustaches of Charlie Chaplin and Groucho Marx, were achieved with Leichner black greasepaint.

Recently, Paris's cultural and commercial establishments have become aware of naturists. The city's first nudist restaurant, O'Naturel, opened in 2017, but closed a year later because of a failure, as the owners put it, to put bums on seats. (The black seat covers were changed for each patron.) The Palais de Tokyo, the city's premiere gallery for contemporary art, also advertised a 2018 visit exclusively for naturists. Three thousand people expressed interest in knowing more but only 116 actually attended. Most found the experience liberating. 'You interact more with the sculptures especially,' said a twenty-three-year-old student. 'In some rooms

where there was music, people moved like they were dancing.' So far, however, there have been no moves to extend the scheme to, for example, the far more populous Louvre.

The boys of *Home Alone* had more to look forward to in the area of nude beaches. Every year, an estimated two million foreigners visit France for purposes of naked tourism, making it the world's number one naturist destination. They almost outnumber the 2.7 million French people who indulge in the same lifestyle at 150 naturist beaches. A few, including one in the Bois de Vincennes, on the eastern side of Paris, are situated near cities, but the majority cluster along the Mediterranean Riviera. The most famous, Cap d'Agde, was designated a naturist resort in 1973. Its *village naturiste* forms a large, self-contained part of the town with hotels, beaches, campsites, shops, bars and restaurants in which nudity is entirely accepted.

Although most enthusiasts insist their pursuits are entirely innocent, Cap d'Agde's reputation for libertine behaviour goes back almost a century, shared with a naturist site on the Île du Levant, offshore from the town of Hyères. Between the wars, Paul Éluard, a core member of the Surrealist movement with an enthusiasm for sex, was a frequent visitor with his second wife, Maria, aka Nusch. Anna, Comtesse de Noailles, described the couple, tanned and glowing after a day on the island, relaxing on the terrace of her villa above Hyères as Éluard read aloud from the poems of Baudelaire; *l'après-midi d'un sensualist* (the afternoon of a sensualist).

A decade earlier, Éluard had been instrumental in introducing members of the Parisian intellectual elite to some less familiar pleasures of the Riviera, reporting excitedly from Marseilles on his discovery of pornographic cinema, and recruiting them for another enthusiasm, *le partouze*, defined as 'a party during which the participants (whose number generally exceeds four) practise the exchange of partners and engage in collective and simultaneous sexual activities'.

At that time, Éluard and his first wife Gala shared a *ménage à trois* with painter Max Ernst. In July 1929, Éluard and Gala travelled to Dalí's home in Cadaqués in Spain with gallerist Camille Goemans, his wife, and Georgette, wife of painter René Magritte. Gala may have subliminally signalled her availability, since from the moment they met, Dalí was smitten.

Gala found herself drawn to the timid but beautiful young Spaniard and encouraged his attentions, letting him sketch her as she reclined almost naked on the beach or bent over a hotel railing. Dalí's studio filled with drawings of her back and buttocks. Éluard watched helplessly as her interest progressed beyond thoughts of a casual *partouze*. When the others returned to Paris, she remained with Dalí, with whom she shared the rest of her life, leaving Éluard to console himself with Baudelaire, Nusch and the Île du Levant.

PÉTANQUE
THE FRENCH GAME

In the Jardin du Luxembourg, where Henri Matisse, Jacques-Louis David and John Singer Sargent once painted (and where, during the Occupation, the Luftwaffe's Western Command made itself comfortable, swimming in the Medici Fountain and digging up the lawns to plant cabbages and potatoes) one no longer sees, as William Faulkner described in his novel *Sanctuary*, people playing croquet. 'In the sad half-light of the chestnut trees,' he wrote, 'the dry shock of the balls and the joyful cries of the children had something of the noble and fleeting melancholy of autumn.'

The chestnuts remain, and there's still an echo of that autumnal *clack clack*, though no longer from a croquet mallet. Instead, the park has two pitches for the playing of *pétanque*, the French version of *boules*. One lies just behind the Musée de Luxembourg and the park's Orangerie, the other, shaded by ancient *marrons* (chestnuts), in a secluded corner next to former tea rooms, now an exhibition space.

Every French holiday home, in the clutter at the back of a cupboard or the bottom of a toy chest, has a set of metal *boules* in their leather carrying harness. Few games are older because few are, superficially at least, simpler. The Romans played with balls of clay. Before that, people used round stones, or hard, unripe fruit, and on the roughest of ground. The less smooth, in fact, the better, since a skilful player exploits the terrain, aiming at a jutting pebble that will kick his ball against that of his opponent and send it skittering far from the marble-sized *cochonnet* (jack).

Classic *boules* requires a green 40m long, and players are allowed a three-step run before releasing the ball. But in 1910, at La Ciotat, near Marseilles, a local café owner, Ernest Pitiot, took pity on his friend

Jules Lenoir who suffered from rheumatism, and adapted the game to accommodate him, halving the play area and allowing the player to stand still for the throw. Locals called this version *pieds tanqués* (feet planted), or, in Provençal, *pètancat*.

Today, the Fédération Française de Pétanque et Jeu Provençal has over 300,000 members. The Mondial la Marseillaise à Pétanque and Trophée des Villes competitions attract large crowds and are broadcast live on national television. There's also a professional circuit, Masters of Pétanque, and since 1985, the Confédération Mondiale des Sports de Boules has been lobbying to make it an Olympic sport.

None of that counts for anything here. A sign warns that only members of the Amicale Sportive du Jardin du Luxembourg are permitted to play. Coats hang neatly a rack provided, next to the dark green-painted kiosk inside which, in numbered boxes, the *boules* of regular players, made to order and calibrated precisely to their taste, remain between matches. The men stand solemnly at the lower end of the play area, sometimes crouching for a moment, the better to assess the ground between them and the cluster of bright metal balls.

Only a few Paris pitches rival the Luxembourg sites. One is on Place Dauphine, on the Île de la Cité, in the middle of the Seine. At lunchtimes, men from the nearby *Monnaie de Paris* (Paris Mint) gather there, joined by others from publishers Gallimard and Editions de Minuit and *avocats* from the Palais de Justice. Commissaire Maigret (had he existed, other than in the pages of Georges Simenon's books) might have watched them from his office in the Prefecture on Quai des Orfèvres.

Pétanque players don't hesitate to protect what they see as their right, privileged by custom, to use certain pieces of ground. In 2022, a poster displayed all over Paris showed a *pétanquer* in typical soft *casquette* (flat hat), crouched, about to launch his *boule*. '*Touche pas à mon CLAP*' (Don't touch my CLAP), it warned.

Club Lepic Abbesses Pétanque – CLAP – is Montmartre's longest-established *pétanque* association. Its 257 members – boasting, they point out, an exceptionally large proportion of women – range in age from twelve to ninety. For decades, play has taken place on public land leased from the council. The eight *pistes* get most use at weekends and in good weather, but are often deserted the rest of the time – cue for the *mairie* (municipal hall) to approach developers. When a hotel company expressed interest, CLAP members protested. There were marches, petitions, reports on television and in the press. The issue still simmers.

Pétanque feeds the French love of drama. No need to know the state of play, or even the rules. Tension resides in the thud of metal on earth, the clang of a well-placed throw, the murmur of disappointment at the unlucky ricochet or the repeated clacking together of *boules* to applaud.

WAR OF THE WORDS
FRENCH VS ENGLISH

When it comes to vocabulary, French doesn't score very high. English has about six times more words. You would expect the French to redress the balance by cribbing from other tongues, as does English. In the field of food alone, where would English be without *soufflé, entrée, banquet, bouquet, sauté* or *sauce*? Not to mention *maître d', gourmet, connoisseur, restaurant* and *chef*? The Académie française is the institution in charge of defining and protecting the French language, with its headquarters in the Institut de France building in Paris. It was officially established in 1635, and comprises forty members, known as *les immortels* (the immortals). Perhaps this is why the French are less inclined to adopt words, preferring to invent new ones. Hence *ordinateurs* rather than computers, *logiciels* instead of programs, *claviers*, not keyboards, and a *souris* instead of a mouse.

Some traffic does take place between the two tongues. A sort of *pidgin* called Franglais, first identified in 1955 by an Argentinian journalist but given official recognition in 1959 by *France-Soir* writer Maurice Rat, became so widespread following the 1964 book *Parlez-vous franglais?* by René Étiemble that the leading dictionaries *Larousse* and *Petit Robert* now list annually those foreign words and phrases that have crept into the language and should be regarded as permanent residents, next to *burger, taxi, cowboy, weekend, brunch, jazz* and *football.* If you are attracted to someone, it's now permissible to say that rather than a *béguin,* you have *un crush.* And if, at the other end of the emotional spectrum, you expunge all trace of them from your metaverse, you have *se faire ghoster.* These transfers are relatively straightforward, others less so. Why *zèbre* for a child prodigy? Nobody seems to know.

Interview is in common usage, as are *cool, gang, cookie, bike, sport* and *parking.* Any adhesive tape, whatever the brand, is *scotch.* For a while, *le drugstore* was among the most fashionable establishments on the Champs-Élysées, but the phrase has long since disappeared, along with the institution from which it took its name. *Pub* did survive, however – and who knew that *happy hour* would also be embraced?

Other words have found a home but become twisted in transit. *Pullover* became simply *pull,* any basketball shoe/ sand shoe/ sneaker/ runner is *un basket,* and dry cleaning, whether it involves steam ironing or not, is *le pressing.* The Académie française, which periodically laments the decline in the classic tongue of Proust and Flaubert, no longer bothers to protest these inclusions, knowing that changing fashion will erase them soon enough. Terms that arrived with the Covid-19 pandemic have already disappeared, mostly unlamented – except perhaps *vaccinodrome* for vaccination centre, which may survive.

Not long ago, every French kid spoke Verlan, a private language related to the Pig Latin of the 1920s. Verlan has its origin in the phrase *à l'envers* (back to front), because *l'envers* backwards sounds a little like *verlan.* In Verlan, *merci* became *cimer, femme* was *meuf.* As Arab backwards was *bar,* young Arabs began identifying themselves as *beur* (*beurre* – butter), so white kids called themselves *margarines.*

There's a larger question which philologists are loath to address. Why, when so many other European nations lie closer than Britain, do so few of their words find their way into French? True, an afternoon nap is *une sieste* and pizza still *pizza,* not *tarte italienne,* but why, for instance, aren't

some of the most-used German words in English also common in French? *Ou sont kindergarten, iceberg, wunderkind, angst, zeitgeist, doppelganger* and *poltergeist*?

Periodically, there is a discussion about which French words might profitably be adopted into English. Candidates include *smoking* for dinner jacket and *slip* for underpants. *Branché* – connected or plugged in – is favoured to replace hip or cool, and *feuilleton* – literally a collection of leaves – to supplant soap opera. *Fiston* has a sharper edge than kid. And is there a more beguiling endearment than *ma biche* – my doe?

And somewhere there should be room for *flâner*; the practice of walking city streets alone, without aim or direction, simply for the pleasure of it. The French invented it, laid down rules for its performance and refined it to the state it enjoys today. Strolling or ambling don't quite fit. Only *flânerie* captures the insouciance, the sense of *joie de vivre*.

And, yes, it *does* require a *circonflexe*. Get used to it.

DOGS, AND WHAT THEY LEAVE BEHIND

F rance is a country for dogs. More than sixty breeds originated here, ranging from the distinctively trimmed poodle, shaved originally to facilitate this hunting animal squirming through thick hedges, to the miniature French bulldog. In 2021, France had an estimated 7.5 million dogs. A quarter of the population kept one or more in their household. Only in the United States is proportion higher. French legislators, eager to accommodate this important segment of the population, went so far as to assign them a special status. It was among the first nations to criminalize the mistreatment of domestic or captive animals, and in 1976 passed a law acknowledging they possessed a form of intelligence, and should not be used for medical experiments and product testing.

French cinema followed suit, with such films as the 1989 *Baxter*, which sees the world through the eyes of a malevolent-looking white bull terrier, whose thoughts, dispassionate when it comes to humans, we hear in voice-over. In 1997, comic Alain Chabat achieved a *coup* in *Didier,* in which a Labrador miraculously becomes a man, but with all the canine attributes, from furious devotion to his master to a genius for ball games that turn him into an inspired but puzzlingly inarticulate football star.

Why so many dogs in France? Sociologists put it down to its status as an essentially rural nation. Traditionally, each farmer had at least one canine companion. Every hunter kept a retriever, and any gentleman would naturally have a pedigree pooch. Even living in a Paris apartment, a dog conferred a sense of status, while a wife found companionship in her little *toutou* (a childish word for a dog). If she went shopping, it went also, often carried in a handbag. In a café or restaurant, it lay under the table, fed the occasional tidbit.

Not everyone shared this enthusiasm. City-dwellers, in particular, criticized the tendency of dogs to defecate wherever the urge overtook them. With so many apartments and relatively few green spaces, this inevitably meant the pavement. Technically, owners could be fined up to €500 for failing to clean up after their animals, but proving the offence could be difficult, and courts had better things to do.

For a city that spent more per capita on sanitation than any city in Europe, the dog droppings in Paris were a continual embarrassment. It tried

pasting vinyl cut-outs, dog-shaped, to the pavement, pointedly close to the gutter. Nobody took notice. A series of posters stressed that the disabled were at a disproportionately greater risk from stepping into it, but images of the blind, aged and otherwise less able caught in mid-pratfall, like most appeals to Parisians' better nature, brought nothing but derision.

In 1982, Jacques Chirac, then mayor, introduced the Caninette, a mobile strike force of motorcycles fitted with vacuum cleaners. Riders in green jumpsuits and white helmets roamed the city, pouncing on steaming heaps and sucking them into a receptacle behind the seat. Immediately christened the *motocrotte* – *crotte* means turd – the scheme was universally derided, particularly after it was found that the fleet of seventy vehicles cleaned up only 20 per cent of droppings but cost $15 million a year to maintain. It was belatedly abandoned in 2002, although it continued to patrol regional Montpellier.

Resignedly, Parisians developed a form of side-scan radar to spot droppings, and a swivel-and-glide manoeuvre, reminiscent of the tango, to avoid a skid. Deciding, philosophically, that, as long as encountering the stuff was inevitable, they might as well benefit from the experience, they also revived a superstition that to have stepped in it with your left foot brought good luck.

Tourists objected not only to the mess, but also to dogs being allowed in shops and restaurants, however docile they may be. As complaints increased, more and more shop-keepers and restaurateurs installed tie-up points outside 'For our four-legged friends'. High rents, smaller apartments, more vigilant landlords and the rising cost of meat saw an end to such massive breeds as St Bernards, Great Danes, wolfhounds and their copious droppings. Jack Russells, Yorkshire Terriers and Chihuahuas took their place.

But outside Paris, large dogs remained popular, encouraging some cities to impose draconian measures. Béziers, in the far south-west, required owners to supply a sample of an animal's saliva if they wished to walk them on the leafy downtown streets. Any mess left behind was DNA tested, and the owner fined. Impatient with the slowness of this process, radicals suggested a more extreme solution. Rather than penalizing individual transgressors, why not accumulate each month's harvest, select a dog owner at random, and deliver the entire steaming heap to their door?

INDEX

ABOUT THE AUTHOR

John Baxter was born in Australia but has lived in Paris for the past thirty years. He has published biographies of Federico Fellini, Luis Buñuel, Steven Spielberg, Woody Allen, Stanley Kubrick, George Lucas and Robert De Niro, as well many books about life in France, including the classic *The Most Beautiful Walk in the World: A Pedestrian in Paris* and the award-winning *The Perfect Meal: In Search of the Lost Tastes of France*. When not writing, John leads literary walking tours of Paris.

Quarto

First published in 2024 by
Frances Lincoln Publishing,
an imprint of The Quarto Group.
One Triptych Place,
London, SE1 9SH,
United Kingdom
T (0)20 7700 6700
www.quarto.com

A catalogue record for this book is available from
the British Library.

ISBN 978-0-7112-9658-9
Ebook ISBN 978-0-7112-9659-6

10 9 8 7 6 5 4 3 2 1

Design by Masumi Briozzo

Printed in China